A LEGION OF DEVILS

Produced in the Republic of South Carolina by

SHOTWELL PUBLISHING LLC
Post Office Box 2592
Columbia, So. Carolina 29202

www.ShotwellPublishing.com

Cover Design: Hazel's Dream
SC State seal image courtesy of the S.C. Historical Society.

ISBN-13: 978-0997939361
ISBN-10: 0997939362

10 9 8 7 6 5 4 3 2 1

A LEGION OF DEVILS

Sherman in South Carolina

Karen Stokes

SHOTWELL PUBLISHING

Columbia, South Carolina

CONTENTS

INTRODUCTION

"He was visited by a legion of devils, not by men."

AFTER COMPLETING HIS DESTRUCTIVE "March to the Sea" through Georgia, General William T. Sherman occupied the city of Savannah in December 1864. He then turned his eyes toward his next objective, South Carolina. In his report concerning the fall of Savannah, Sherman informed General Ulysses S. Grant that he intended to "smash South Carolina—all to pieces." His strategy was to divide and confuse Confederate forces by marching on the capital city of the state, Columbia, and destroying as many railroad lines en route as possible. He had no intention of attacking Augusta, Georgia, or Charleston, South Carolina. He did not consider Charleston an important military target since it was already, as he put it, "a mere desolated wreck." His strategy was also to break the morale of South Carolinians and the Confederate Army.

Shortly before General Sherman invaded South Carolina, he wrote to his superior officer General Henry W. Halleck, "The whole army is crazy to be turned loose in Carolina." His army for this campaign consisted of over 60,000 troops accompanied by a train of 2,500 wagons carrying ammunition and food supplies that could not be foraged off the country. There were also 600 ambulances, and each corps also carried along pontoon bridges for the crossing of waterways. In his excellent book on Sherman, *Merchant of Terror*, John B. Walters wrote: "The Federal troops, as they had done in Georgia, divided into several columns and marched by different roads to specified rendezvous points. This splitting of forces mystified the Confederate generals in South Carolina and Augusta, as it had in Georgia, and again caused them to separate their small forces. In consequence, Sherman's army marched through the middle, encountering little or no effective opposition from the Confederate troops. Confederate Generals Joe Wheeler, Wade Hampton and Hardee withdrew their forces consistently and burned the bridges behind them as the impetus of Sherman's heavy columns carried the invading Federal troops relentlessly farther and farther into South Carolina."

The march through Georgia had been relatively easy for Sherman's army, but they found it harder going through South Carolina, moving through the swampy lowlands swollen by rains, and crossing rivers at flood stage. It was hard work to move heavy artillery carriages and wagons through mud and water, and the army laid down many miles of corduroy (or log) roads. They also constructed thousands of feet of pontoon bridges over waterways.

In January 1865, Sherman's forces gathered at Beaufort, South Carolina, and during that month a few of his brigades moved a little farther inland into the Lowcountry. Beaufort, a town south of Charleston near the coast, had been captured early November 1861 and remained in Union hands until the end of the war. The occupying Federal army allowed the slaves in the area a measure of freedom, and teachers came down from the North to begin to educate them, but the Federal soldiers frequently mistreated them. A newspaper correspondent for the *New York Tribune* reported in its issue of December 7, 1861, that "one enterprising and unscrupulous [Federal] officer was caught in the act of assembling a cargo of Negroes for transportation and sale in Cuba. "In 1862, Esther Hill Hawks , a Northern female physician and teacher who worked for the Freedmen's Aid Society, noted in her diary how disgracefully the black people of the Beaufort area were treated by the Federal soldiers. She observed that "no colored woman was safe from the brutal lusts of the soldiers," and that they were not punished for their offenses.

General Sherman left Savannah and arrived at Beaufort by steamer on January 23. While his troops were there, they manifested much hostility toward the many black people who lived in the occupied area. Sherman's soldiers stole from them, destroyed their property, and taunted them with racial slurs. About this time, General Oliver O. Howard, Sherman's second in command, wrote to another Union general that his soldiers were "abusing their women." There were also some violent confrontations between some of Sherman's soldiers and the black Union troops at Beaufort. According to Tom Elmore's book *A Carnival of Destruction,* Sherman's soldiers killed at least two black men and injured several others before they left Beaufort.

One of Sherman's officers, Colonel Oscar L. Jackson of the 63rd Ohio Infantry Regiment, observed how the soldiers of Sherman's army treated the blacks in his diary: "I am grieved to see many of our soldiers treat them with the greatest unkindness and try to make them think they are to be, and if they follow us will be, again enslaved ... we have soldiers so degraded and low born as to plunder the houses of the blacks of the last mouthful of food and every valuable and take pleasure in insulting and molesting them when they meet them."

By the first of February 1865, the main advance had begun, and Sherman's army moved into South Carolina and began to cut a broad swath of destruction across the state, committing not only arson and pillage, but also murder and other serious offenses. Having been the first state to secede from the union, South Carolina was singled out for particularly savage treatment by the Northern army, and in my book *South Carolina Civilians in Sherman's Path,* I chronicle the harrowing experiences of many people who encountered these soldiers.

Sherman's principal target in South Carolina, the city of Columbia, was located in the heart of the state. When you hear or read about the burning of Columbia, you are often told that the origin of the fire is a historical mystery that can't be conclusively solved, or that the fires were actually initiated by the evacuating Confederate troops, or even by the citizens of Columbia themselves. None of this is true.

In her recent book *Sherman's Flame and Blame Campaign,* Patricia McNeely investigated why such falsehoods about the burning of Columbia have persisted over the decades, despite the fact that she had "read an avalanche of eye-witness accounts that leave no doubt that General William T. Sherman's drunken troops burned Columbia." Tom Elmore, who spent over a decade and a half researching Sherman's South Carolina campaign, commented in his book *A Carnival of Destruction,* "While there exists a plethora of evidence that Sherman's men were the ones primarily responsible for the city's destruction, it is unlikely Sherman apologists will anytime soon abandon their argument supporting his innocence."

Before Columbia was surrendered, some cotton bales had been placed in the middle of Main Street "in order to be burned to prevent their falling into the possession of the invaders," as it was stated in an official report compiled by a committee of Columbia citizens. The Confederate commanders, including General Wade Hampton, were afraid this might endanger the town and issued explicit orders that the cotton should not be burned, and subsequently the Confederate forces withdrew from Columbia, leaving the cotton bales in the streets untouched.

Patricia McNeely wrote of this: "The cotton was in the middle of just part of the block with an interval of several feet between the bales and the pavement and houses on either side ... The dirt streets were 100-feet wide in most places ... and muddy from the all-night rain." As Sherman's forces filled the city, some of the cotton bales were set afire, some said from the cigars of the soldiers, but these smaller fires were completely extinguished by mid-afternoon. The fires that destroyed much of the city did not begin until about 8 p.m. in the evening. The following day, Sherman attributed the burning of the city to his drunken troops. Not long afterward, however, he claimed that General Wade Hampton was responsible for the city's destruction and that his men had set the cotton on fire before departing. Sherman made this charge about Hampton in his official report to his superior General Halleck. Ten years later, when Sherman's memoirs were published, he admitted that he had laid the blame on Gen. Hampton merely to shake the confidence of the South Carolina people in their hero Hampton.

Colonel Oscar L. Jackson wrote this in his diary the day after the burning of Columbia:

February 18th. I went over to the city this morning and found it mostly in ruins ... It is no exaggeration to say that the city is burned. I believe it was not done by order but there seems to be a general acquiescence in the work as a fit example to be made of the capital ... It is generally understood that at dark our drunken soldiery fired it in numerous places. Perhaps the brigade on duty in the city made some efforts to put out the fires, but I do not think you could have gotten enough men in the army disposed to stop it to have effected anything. A few soldiers were so drunk that they were burnt. There were no residences of noted rebels left unburned except a few occupied by our Generals as headquarters, and several prominent generals were burned out a time or two.

Later, Jackson noted: "There was a recklessness by the soldiery in South Carolina that they never exhibited before and a sort of general 'don't care' on the part of the officers. South Carolina can show wounds equal to any state that has suffered from the war."

William A. Nicholson was a clerk in the Confederate hospital located within the buildings of the South Carolina College in Columbia. Nicolson and Surgeon A. W. Thompson remained behind with their "180 or 190 sick and dying" patients after the Confederate forces withdrew from the city, and in a memoir, recalling a letter he wrote to his parents as Sherman's army marched in, Nicholson recorded the following:

> In the letter to my parents I depicted in as strong language as I could command the brutal conduct of the commanding general in allowing his army the privileges of the city under the circumstances. I never have believed that General Sherman issued an order for the burning of the city, but as a general who was familiar with the sentiment of his men, as openly expressed, what they would do when they took the city, he certainly took no steps to prevent its destruction. I heard Dr. Goodwyn, then mayor of the city, tell Dr. Thompson that General Sherman told him to go to bed, that the city would not be destroyed, when at the moment his men were engaged in setting fire to the homes of helpless women and children. As an eyewitness to those awful scenes, a more bald, untruthful statement was never uttered than the one said to have been made by General Sherman—that General Hampton burned Columbia.

Nicholson movingly described the terrible night of Columbia's destruction and the plight of the sick men in the hospital:

From the time the troops passed the College campus, till about 5 o'clock, nothing of very special interest occurred. It is true fires in different parts of the city had occurred during the day; but it was not until after dark on the 17th of February that the work of fiendish destruction began. The troops from the various camps began to pour into the city like the locusts, the fires becoming more numerous as darkness set in. Dr. Thompson and I took our position in the cupola of the College building to watch the progress of the flames. We saw Federal soldiers plainly setting fire to the State House, the light from the burning building making it light as day. While viewing this awful scene the cry reached us that the hospital buildings had caught fire. The wind at this time was blowing furiously, and the burning embers were falling thick as hail. Before reaching the ground the cry of fire had reached the ears of the helpless and dying men in the hospital. These poor creatures were crawling on their hands and knees from the building to avoid what they feared would be a more awful death than the one which it was only a question of a very brief period would relieve them from their mental and physical sufferings.

The scene that presented itself to me at that hour can never be effaced from my memory. The sight of these brave, dying men crawling in their helplessness from the different wards, the burning embers falling so fast that it required the exertions of an active person to keep their clothing from being burned on their persons, the screams of women and children, houses falling, the yells of the drunken soldiers; to me it sounded then—and does now, on looking back on that night—that no picture by pen or brush could possibly be drawn of the infernal regions that would strike greater terror to the beholder...

Thompson and Nicholson soon discovered that it was not the hospital building that was on fire, but the roof of a neighboring house. With the help of some soldiers under the command of the Federal provost marshal, who learned that some United States soldiers were also in the hospital, the roof fire was extinguished.

Like William A. Nicholson, many South Carolinians left behind a written record of what they saw and experienced in South Carolina during the fateful winter of 1865. This book draws together some of the most compelling and significant eyewitness accounts and recollections of that time, including testimonies collected by Wade Hampton, who responded to Sherman's slanderous accusations with a scathing indictment of his war crimes. Also included is a timeline documenting most of the significant incidents of the Federal army's invasion of South Carolina from January through March 1865.

CHAPTER ONE

SOUTH CAROLINA WOMEN IN THE WAR

THE FOLLOWING ACCOUNTS are taken from a collection of personal narratives entitled *Our Women in the War*, published in 1885. The first, "In the Track of Sherman's Army," is a memoir by Mrs. Alfred P. Aldrich, who lived at a plantation close to Barnwell, South Carolina. The town of Barnwell was put to the torch by Sherman's cavalry commander, General Hugh Judson Kilpatrick, a little over a week before the Federal forces captured Columbia. The second account, "The Sack of Columbia," describes the experiences of Mrs. Sarah Ann Rou Crittenden (1839-1911) during the burning of that city.

In the Track of Sherman's Army, by Mrs. A. P. Aldrich, "The Oaks," Barnwell, S.C.

Some months ago the name of Gen. William Tecumseh Sherman, as a fit nominee for President of the United States by the Republican party, appeared in the papers. When I saw this notice it made the blood course rapidly through my veins, and my heart beat fast, bringing vividly to my mind the ordeal through which I and my helpless children passed when the left wing of the army marched through Barnwell in that memorable February of 1865. And I said to myself, can it be possible that man will ever have it in his power to oppress Southern women and children again? Although over three score years have left their mark upon my face and form, I then determined to avail myself of the columns of THE

1

WEEKLY NEWS AND COURIER to add one more contributor to my Southern sisters "Our Women in the War," to put on record some of the events which transpired at that time in our home and grounds. Hence my narrative—"In the Track of Sherman's Army."

Early in the morning of the 5th of February we heard the anticipated sounds of a death-knell, the bombarding of the fortifications on the Salkehatchie, three miles below our town. I have often thought since what mirth that structure, a mere mole-hill, must have created in the great Union army, as they looked upon our puny efforts to stay their march even for one hour. The first detachment that entered the town was Kilpatrick's Cavalry, which must have been some time in advance of the infantry. He made headquarters at the largest and best house, in the centre of town, leaving his soldiers to range for miles around the country, committing the most ruthless depredations.

It was a party of this cavalry who, crossing the beautiful little stream which separates our place, a half-mile beyond, from the town, came dashing up the avenue as if they were afraid some of their comrades might outstrip them and secure the booty they hoped to grasp. As I stood upon the piazza and looked at these first "blue-coats" approaching, I will not deny that my heart sank within me, and I felt like falling, for I remembered the horrible accounts we had for months been listening to of the brutal treatment of the army to the women of Georgia in their march from Atlanta to Savannah. The courage of which I had always felt myself possessed, I confess, forsook me then and I prayed to God to protect me and my little ones from the invaders. The first of the soldiers who rushed into the house seemed only intent on searching for food, and when the safe was opened to them,

ATE LIKE HUNGRY WOLVES.

So soon, however, as they were satisfied, their tramp through the house began. By this time they were pouring in at every door, and without asking to have bureaus and wardrobes opened, broke with their bayonets every lock, tearing out the contents, in hunting for gold, silver, and jewels, all of which had been sent off weeks before, and in the burning of the Convent lost! Finding nothing to satisfy their cupidity so far, they began turning over mattresses, tearing open feather-beds, and scattering the contents in the wildest confusion.

The infantry soon appeared and were ten days and nights passing through in detachments. During that time their tents were pitched all around us, and our park lit up by their camp fires, and our yard and home filled with hundreds of rude soldiers. When one swarm departed, another "more hungry" for spoil would file in. And so we lived for days and nights, with guns and bayonets flashing in our faces, and the coarse language of this mass of ruffians sounding in our ears. Having no one to send to headquarters for guards, we were often subjected to worse treatment than our more fortunate neighbors who lived immediately in town.

One day a wretch who looked as if he had been brought from Sing Sing for the purpose of terrifying women and children, came into my piazza where he was standing surrounded by a more decent crowd than usual, carrying a rope in his hand, with which I learned afterwards he had three times

HUNG UP ONE OF OUR SERVANTS

who had been reported to him as having aided me in hiding my silver. Here I will state that I permitted none of our negroes to know anything connected with concealing valuables, from the fact that I was well aware they could by bribes or threats be induced to tell all they knew. Each of the three times that this man suspended poor Frank in the air he would let him down and try to make him confess. Not knowing anything, of course he could not give the coveted information. Frank's neck remains twisted to this day. With the rope shaken in my face, the monster said: "Madame, if you do not tell me in five minutes where your silver is buried I will set fire to your home."

Fortunately I had asked, not long before, a very gentlemanly looking soldier—there were *some* of this class, of whom I shall speak in the course of the narrative—if Gen. Sherman permitted houses occupied by women and children to be burned? and had been told he did not. So I promptly replied to the ruffian.

"You dare not burn my house," I said, "for General Sherman has forbidden it."

Just then I was greatly surprised to hear a voice at my back say: "Let the lady alone; you have no right to insult her after taking everything you could find. As to her silver, I can tell you, it is not here; it has been sent to Camden for safety!"

I turned and looked at the pleasant, humane looking face of this soldier in wonder and gratitude for his timely interference.

Soon my housekeeper came near and whispered: "I told him, and begged him to protect you from the wretch who was threatening you."

This good man stood nobly by us in several trying scenes after, and repeatedly expressed his disapprobation of the war, and his sorrow for what he saw going on around him. Of his sincerity we could only hope.

Some days after, when the vandals were swarming in and around the house, a faithful servant, who had stood by us in many troubles, came to me and said: "Mam, I have with a tub of water followed a soldier under the house and put out the fire four times as soon as he left it, and now he is building one under the parlor, and swears he will blow my brains out if I destroy his work again."

"You have done all you can Moses," I said, "don't endanger your own life. I will see what I can do."

As I went down the front steps I saw an officer—by his uniform—entering the gate, and ran to him for help.

When I told him what was being done, he seemed indignant, and asked me to show him the man.

I led the way to where the smoke began to burst from under the house, and both of us stooping down saw the man creeping out. The officer ordered him to go back and extinguish the fire, and looking up quickly, he recognized one in authority, and obeyed.

When he came out and stood upright, I exclaimed: "That is the man who came an hour ago and offered to stand guard to protect my home."

The officer—he was one of the few gentlemen I had met in that fearful crowd—said in an excited and indignant tone: "Give me your name," at the same time taking out a note book and pencil from his pockets.

The name was given and put down.

"To what company do you belong? And to what regiment?"

Each was answered and recorded.

"And you were the guard for this lady?"

"I had no authority to do so," he said, "I only offered of my own head."

"So much the greater reason why you should have been faithful. You shall answer to Gen. Sherman for this act. Go up to headquarters, sir."

Now this may have been the last of it—probably was; but the officer looked like a man who meant what he said. At any rate it was most comforting to feel myself in the presence of

A GENTLEMAN AND A PROTECTOR.

A few days after, a kind hearted lieutenant, as he came up our avenue, saw the housekeeper going out the front gate, and said:

"Madam, are you leaving your home filled with soldiers? Why it will soon be in flames over your head."

"I am not the mistress; she is inside. I am going to try and get a guard at headquarters."

"Go back and help to save your home," he kindly said, "I will procure a guard for you."

Mrs. E. came and reported his warning, and said: "You follow them on the lower floor, while I go up-stairs." She was none too soon, for as she reached the landing, she heard a match scratched

6

and great laughter. Running into a chamber beyond, she found a party of the "Boys"—this seemed to be a pet name for the privates by their officers—surrounding the bed, on which they had piled up books and papers, and applied the match. She sprang forward and scattered the combustibles on the floor, exclaiming: "My God, do you intend to burn us up!"

This greatly amused them, one fellow saying: "No, we are only making a fire to warm by."

The same day my seamstress ran in to tell me a fire had been kindled in a small house within five steps of our dwelling, in which was kept cotton for spinning our negro clothes, with yarn and other materials most suitable for effecting a quick conflagration. I flew out, and saw two men jumping from the door, well nigh suffocated by the smoke they had created. Without speaking, I rushed by them, and with a sley used for weaving cloth scattered and threw out of the door the burning cotton and yarn. A few moments later, nothing could have saved our house.

These are a few only of the incidents which kept us on the watch day and night to counteract the attempts of these incendiaries ...

I think it was the day following that a fresh party, searching for valuables, found the coat in which one of our only two sons, a Lieutenant in the Company of Citadel Cadets, 6th Regiment of South Carolina Volunteers, had been desperately wounded at Trevelyan Station.

This coat was carried up to "headquarters," by orders, I presume, and that afternoon an officer, speaking to Mrs. E. said: "That lieutenant must have been badly wounded, to judge by the condition of the coat, the shoulder of which is all torn to pieces."

We never knew till then that the coat was in their possession.

When asked if they would not return it to us, the officer replied: "Oh! no; we like to keep all these little things."

He inquired where the wounded "Confederate" was, and on being told he had gone up to Augusta to report to the hospital, laughed and said: "He is a lucky fellow." Meaning, we suppose, that if he had been found here he would have been taken prisoner.

Thus other days and nights went by, and that "left wing" had well nigh passed on to burn Columbia. Here let me say, notwithstanding Gen. Sherman denies that he committed that act of vandalism, his soldiers, right in this house, said, when they heard our three eldest daughters had been sent to the Convent, with most of our valuables: "You had better have kept them at home; they would be safer here, for

COLUMBIA IS TO BE LAID IN ASHES

and as for that Convent, we are bound to get in there, for we hear is concealed in its vaults half the treasures of the rich nabobs of this State."

This—the burning of the city—I thought most likely, judging by my experience of the "fire-fiend" spirit which possessed them. But now I felt distressed about my children, for I had been told that the Catholic Brigade of the Army protected all the Church Institutions in the line of their march through Georgia, and supposed they would do the same in our State. How true, I know not, but it was stated after the destruction of the Convent that this brigade was not permitted to cross over the Congaree until after the city was fired ...

I do not remember the day our town was burned, or the division of the army that accomplished it, but I do remember the spectacle presented the first time I beheld the ruins. All the public buildings were destroyed. The fine brick Courthouse, which cost the State between $12,000 and $15,000, with most of the stores, laid level with the ground, and many private residences, with only the chimneys standing like grim sentinels; the Masonic Hall in ashes. I had always believed that the archives, jewels and sacred emblems of the Order were so reverenced by Masons everywhere, whether belonging to friend or foe, that those wearing the "Blue" would guard the temple of their brothers in "Grey." Not so, however. Nothing in South Carolina was held sacred. All fell under the heel of the oppressor alike.

The picturesque little Town of Barnwell has been greatly admired for its fair old oaks and fine evergreens. It is built upon a hill, at the base of which runs a beautiful clear stream encircling two sides of it ... and here the Federal army, with its thousands of men and horses, slaked their thirst... My beautiful avenue of oaks, which I had transplanted years before, from my childhood's home far away, had been ruthlessly cut down or killed by camp fires kindled at their roots ...

The Sack of Columbia, by Mrs. S. A. Crittenden, of Greenville County, S.C.

The Federal army, under Sherman, lay just on the other side of the Congaree, and the bombarding went on steadily, without, however, doing much damage. Hampton, with a feeble force, was left in command of the defence of the Capital ...

To the women and children of that doomed city things began to look gloomy in the extreme. Many refugees who had come from Charleston, and other parts of the low-country, resumed their flight, seeking safety in the upper districts, nearer the mountains. Many residents of Columbia followed them; in fact, nearly all who could get away fled, leaving their household goods to the mercy of the invaders. Shells and cannon balls have voices of singular persuasiveness to induce non-combatants to "move on," and not many willingly kept reserved seats to listen to their music.

THE BELEAGUERED CITY

On Thursday night there was little sleep in the beleaguered city. I had dressed a day or two before for any emergency, and did not remove my dress for a week. I had taken an apron of strong Scotch ginghams, doubled it up and run casings in it, and into these stowed away important papers belonging to my husband, some money and a few articles of jewelry. This I wore as a bustle and was undisturbed in its possession. Others were not so fortunate. Many had their clothing torn off and their persons searched by the lawless soldiery and the mob who reaped a harvest on that fearful night of February 17, 1865.

On Friday morning, while we were at breakfast, a sound of musketry broke the ominous stillness, and we learned that the Yankees had crossed the river on pontoon bridges, and that the city was virtually in their hands. The mayor and some of the chief municipal officers had gone to Gen. Sherman's headquarters and surrendered our beautiful Capital, and received from him the comforting assurance that Columbia should be as safe as if it had been under Mayor Goodwyn's own administration.

"Some of the public buildings, such as the Arsenal and Armory, will have to be destroyed," said Sherman, "but I will select a calm day for the purpose, and nothing else shall be injured. Go home and sleep in peace, Mr. Mayor, your city shall be safe." How well he kept this promise let Columbia's burning homes, her desolate streets, and her houseless, starving children tell.

THE CITY IN FLAMES

No pen can adequately depict the horrors of the burning of Columbia. Every hearthstone was an altar on which the Yankees sacrificed to their gods—Vengeance and Hatred—and every blazing roof-tree will be a burning record against their wanton cruelty in the day of final count. All day the storm had been gathering. Here and there some outrageous act gave a foretaste of what was in store for the "Rebs" between the setting and rising of the sun.

About 10 o'clock P. M. the signal rockets began to go up, and soon the incendiary fires blazed out. I was told by squads of drunken soldiers, followed by a rabble of drunken and excited negroes, paraded the principal thoroughfares, entering about every fourth house with torch and oil, and soon had blocks and whole streets one mass of living flame.

My husband, being Northern born, though strongly Southern in feeling, many persons thought his house would be spared, therefore the house was packed from basement to attic with the furniture of our neighbors sent hither for protection; but, alas! the Demon of Destruction was no respecter of persons or property, and at 2 o'clock in the morning I took a little bird in its cage, which I could not bear to leave to the flames, in one hand and my little child's hand in the other, and walked out from under our burning roof into the cold and pitiless street. Hundreds, nay thousands were there before me; some not so well off as I, for they were invalids. None of us had any pillow but the frozen ground, nor any covering but the burning heavens.

The terrified lowing of cattle, the frenzied flight of pigeons circling high above their blazing cotes, the ribald jests and brutal assaults of our drunken conquerors, the dun clouds of despair rolling between us and the pitying eye of God, made up a picture whose counterpart can be found only in the regions of the eternally lost.

"VAEVICTIS"

On Saturday morning we took refuge with some kind friends in the suburbs whose house had been overlooked rather than spared and not until Sunday did we venture back to look at the ruins of our once beautiful home.

Oh! the utter, utter desolation of a city in ashes and its people wanderers! Even the very landmarks were lost, and you stood a stranger on your own threshold. Nothing was left but the smokeless chimneys, keeping ward over the widespread ruin. Hundreds of Yankees, with ramrods and bayonets, were prodding the still smoking soil in quest of buried treasure.

On Tuesday morning the blue lines formed and the invaders left Columbia—a city once a synonym of all that was beautiful and elegant—a heap of ruins; her living homeless and scattered, her dead insulted and desecrated. To me the curse of the broken-hearted sounded above their steady tramp and martial music. Confusion and terror went before them and want and despair hovered in their rear. *VaeVictis* may not have been inscribed on their banners, but it was written in characters of blood and living fire on the hearts and homes of a conquered people.

I remember going, a few Sabbaths after the destruction of the city, to one of our ministers. He was one who had been personally abused by the Vandal horde in their mad riot on that fatal night, and a just and holy indignation still burned in his clerical bosom.

"My friends," said he, warming in his discourse, "Let us be faithful in following our Divine Master until we come to the New Jerusalem, the golden city, not a desolate place like this, but ever bright and fair, and I assure you, my friends, there will be no villainous Yankees there." Then remembering that he was pledged to preach a doctrine of forgiveness, he added reluctantly and doubtfully, "Unless they have entirely new hearts."

I could not refrain from adding a mental amen to this sentiment.

Necessity is said to be the mother of invention. If this be true Columbians should have been the most inventive people on the face of the earth during that spring of eighteen hundred and sixty-five, for their needs were certainly great.

Left without shelter, clothing or food, and with no means to obtain either, their condition was indeed deplorable. I heard of many persons sustaining life for several days upon the corn picked up around the feeding troughs of the Yankees' horses.

A lady whom I had known in her days of prosperity came to me, with the tears streaming down her cheeks and said: "If you have anything divide with me—my little children are at home crying for bread."

Alas, I was but little better off.

A SHAMEFUL OUTRAGE

Here let me give you an incident that occurred in our sister State of North Carolina. A surgeon-dentist, a man of position, ability and unquestioned integrity, lived within that broad swathe of desolation cut by the Federal army in its victorious march. He afterwards came to Columbia and from him I heard an account of the shameful outrage.

Years had passed and Columbia, rising from her sackcloth and ashes, had clothed herself anew in the beautiful and strong garments of energy and enterprise. We had accepted our trials ... and were disposed to forgive if not to forget.

Conversing one day with Dr. G., our dentist, he expressed an undying hatred for the men who had caused him so much grief.

"If anybody," said he, "hates the wretches who followed Sherman's army more than I do, it is because his capacity for hating is greater than mine. This is strong language, but I am justified in using it. When Sherman's army passed through my place in North Carolina, some of his camp-followers, in their greedy search for treasure, entered the graveyard, dug up my dead children, opened their coffins, and left their bodies exposed to birds and beast, less vile than they. Tell me to forgive them? Never! My outraged dead, with their mute lips, cry out against it! The desecration of all the nameless bones of my countrymen, left to bleach on our hillsides and valleys, forbid it. Every instinct of my manhood is hatred toward those human jackals."

Chapter Two

McCarter's Eyewitness Account of the Burning of Columbia

THE MANUSCRIPT COLLECTIONS of the Library of Congress include an interesting document entitled the "McCarter Journal." It was written by James Jefferson McCarter (1800-1872), a native of the state of New Jersey. Before becoming a resident of Columbia, South Carolina, he lived in Charleston, where he made a living as a bookseller and was a member of the "Conversation Club" in that city, an association of educated, intellectual gentlemen who met weekly to discuss and debate various subjects.

In Columbia, he was a partner in the business of Bryan & McCarter, booksellers. He was also one of the citizens who accompanied Mayor Goodwyn to an interview with General Sherman after Columbia was burned. In his "Journal," McCarter records many horrific details about the night of the city's destruction and its aftermath, noting for instance, that "The bodies of several females were found in the morning of Saturday stripped naked & with only such marks of violence upon them as would indicate the most detestable of crimes ... the town seemed abandoned to the unrestrained license of the half drunken soldiery to gratify their base passions on the unprotected females of both colors."

The following are some of the most gripping excerpts from McCarter's account.

About ten a.m. I saw the head of two columns marching thro' the main street & soon after I saw the last remnant of Butler's cavalry disappear by the Camden road. About 2 p.m. I conversed with an officer of Blair's staff who had strolled into the neighborhood where I lived & was assured by him that no inhabited house would be disturbed & no private property injured, that all the citizens had to do was to remain at home, & they would not be molested. He had not left me many moments when I saw his men ... pillaging the citizens of their watches & other valuables, presenting their carbines at the heads of men who were supposed to have concealed gold & demanding its instant surrender.

About 1 p.m. a house on the west side of Main Street was on fire, and as the wind was high, it was evident all that part of the city ... must be burned. Still we hoped there would be no further incendiarism. About 4 ½ or 5 p.m. the beautiful places of Gen. Hampton & Mr. Trenholm two or three miles from town, were seen in flames. About 8 p.m. fire could be seen in several places, which as they were considerably distant from each other & all in the upper part of the city & in the quarter from whence the wind blew, we began to think that the destruction of the city was intended. The assurances of the guards which had been placed around the city, both officers & men, that no destruction was intended to private property, prevented the citizens removing out of their houses such articles of clothing, bedding, & kitchen furniture as were indispensable to their comfort & most families lost not only all their furniture but liberal supplies of provisions, laid in by prudent housekeepers, were also destroyed. As soon as it became evident that the city was doomed to destruction, a general effort was made to save something, but all valuable articles which were visible to the light (the light was almost equal to the noonday sun) were snatched from the hands of the owners & their servants & became a prey to the captors.

Bands of men with muskets & carbines penetrated into cellars & into garrets in search of plunder, wrenching open wardrobes & bureaus & ripping open beds in the expectation of finding gold & silver. Liquor having been found in quantities, both officers and soldiers drank to excess & were seen staggering from house to house frantic with excitement, cursing the rebels for causing the war. Whenever guards did their duty property within the dwellings escaped much injury. In many cases they united with the plunderers in the work of pillage & destruction. Whatever had been removed from the burning buildings was deemed lawful prey, & many families who had saved a little clothing or a little food from the flames were robbed by the soldiers of that little ...

The fire had reached from the extreme outskirts of the city, & even beyond the corporate limits on Richardson St. & Main St. to the State house, a distance of a mile & a quarter. The space burnt was, with only here & there a standing house ... about a quarter of a mile in width, by a mile & a quarter in length, & comprised the entire business portion of the city & many of the most costly & best furnished houses .... Of the buildings not hurt, it is no exaggeration to say, not one escaped plundering ...

My own house was not burnt ... I had been visited on Saturday about 12 o'clock noon by the soldiers in the uniform of Federal Cavalry. I had been assured by Lt. McCall of Gen. Blair's or perhaps Gen. Logan's staff that there was no need to have a guard stationed in our houses. Sherman would protect all private property. Lt. McCall had scarcely got out of sight when two cavalry rode up to my house, hitched their horses to the pickets of my ...

fence & rushed up my piazza steps. One of them put his carbine within an inch of my head & exclaimed, "You damned old rebel, give me your watch, or I will blow your damned brains out." I replied that he need not use any violence as I could make no resistance. They followed me into my bedroom where my watch lay upon my bureau & having seized it, the same man who pointed his gun at me before, repeated the action, this time demanding my gold. On my assurance that I had none, the other trooper exclaimed that "they had done pretty well," & picking up a pair of shoes which were in sight, they departed in a hurry & leaving me with the impression they were afraid some of their officers would catch them in their unlawful act.

On Sunday morning I heard a noise in the rear of my lot like the breaking down of a fence & on going out to see I found an officer with an axe knocking the boards off the fence & rolling out a barrel of flour, which I had placed in the garden with some other provisions so that we might have some food if the house was burnt. This officer said to me "General Sherman has heard you have some very choice wheat flour & has sent me for a couple of barrels." Of course he took the barrels tho I did not believe he had any authority from Sherman ...

It is not easy to form a definite opinion as to the intentions of a commanding general respecting Columbia. In company with Mayor Goodwyn& about half a dozen citizens, I visited the General Sunday morning & found him courteous, affable & apparently well pleased with his success. He had the good sense not to make any excuse or apologize for the destruction of the town. He was evidently well versed in the political history of parties & alluded to the attempt of the South to force slavery on Kansas as the most important fact which had alienated from the South her warmest friends ... He expressed himself in favor of domestic servitude & only objected to what he called "plantation slavery." The committee of citizens listened to the excited & exultant general without reply ... forbearing to argue with a victorious commander at the head of 60,000 bayonets. To each of the propositions of the mayor he gave a hearty consent. The delivery of such provisions as remained in the depots, turning over to the mayor some salt & a number of cattle, which had been taken from the citizens, to be distributed among the destitute.

We had to learn the humiliating lesson of being suppliant for a morsel of our own bread & for our own meat to a general of the despised Yankee race, upon whom so recently we had poured out the most contemptuous antipathy. In the course of that Sabbath morning, I had encountered Gen. Howard, Blair ... & several officers of inferior ranks. They all wore a serious & even saddened aspect as if ashamed of the mischief they had been compelled to do. Sherman alone appeared flushed with victory, & made no effort to conceal his exultation. He occasionally made remarks bordering on the facetious which were strangely out of place or harmony with his suffering & sorrowful auditory ...

It is difficult to reconcile Gen. Sherman's official report of the causes which led to the burning of Columbia with his conversation with the mayor & committee of citizens that Sabbath morning. I was present at the interview & have recently refreshed my memory by comparing notes with Dr. Goodwyn. On the afternoon of Friday Dr. Goodwyn called on Sherman at his headquarters to consult with him as to the best method of preserving order. It was near night & the mayor naturally felt very anxious about the safety of the city. Many of the privates & some of the officers had been heard to use threatening language, & the fears not only of the mayor but of most of the inhabitants were greatly excited. Sherman in his bluff implusive manner said, "Go to bed, Mr. Mayor, you are tired & worn out. I will take care of your town a great deal better than you can." The mayor having lost two or three nights' sleep, did as he was advised & he tried to rest, only to be aroused by the firing of his own dwelling from which he & his family escaped with scarce any clothing ...

At our interview with Sherman Sunday morning he seemed to remember his promise of protection. He said, "Doctor you brought all this on yourselves. There was too much liquor in your town & your people distributed too much of it to my soldiers. It is all your fault."

There is no doubt Columbia was set on fire in many places by Sherman's soldiery. Many of them had determined before they came to destroy the town & revel in its destruction. It is not to be supposed (tho many do entertain the supposition I fear) that Sherman ordered the burning of Columbia, tho I doubt if he took any precautions to prevent it ...

I saw 10 regiments of one division passing, numbering each at least five hundred men & these were but a small portion of Sherman's troops which entered the city, while I doubt Beauregard's whole force amounted to 4,000. Indeed the impression Sherman made on me & on many of our citizens was that he could go anywhere he pleased. The wagon trains seemed all in fine order ...

I can truly say I <u>saw</u> no act of personal violence during the occupation of the city by Sherman's troops. But I fear there were many, such acts resting on the testimony of most respectable citizens. Certain it is that soon after the pillage began the frightened negro women sought earnestly protection & places of refuge against the lustful soldiery & even abandoned their little property to get under the protection of some efficient guard. The bodies of several females were found in the morning of Saturday stripped naked &with only such marks of violence upon them as would indicate the most detestable of crimes. In an army of 30 or 40 thousand men there must have been some mere brutes who took the occasion when the town seemed abandoned to the unrestrained license of the half drunken soldiery to gratify their base passions on the unprotected females of both colors. I would cast a veil over this part of the history of the fall of Columbia.

Both officers and men seem to vie with each other in punishing this town for the prominent part she bore in the rebellion (revolution). They were all deeply imbued with the sentiment of "Union." "This glorious Union" was constantly on their lips, like the crusaders under Peter the Hermit they wanted to reestablish the Union even if by doing so they annihilated the present population. So the crusaders wished to plant the cross of Christ on the holy sepulcher even if it cost the lives of myriads of men, women & children. This strange fanaticism pervaded the whole army from Sherman down to the meanest private in the ranks.

One officer left a note on a blank leaf of a school book, in which he stated "In the year 1865 this great rebellion would be crushed out, & peace and harmony & good will would be restored between the North & South." As if the burning of our towns & the pillage of our houses, the destruction of our implements of agriculture, our mills, foundries was the best method of restoring peace, harmony & good will between these contending sections. (The sole object of Sherman's campaign was to destroy the resources of the South so they could no longer continue the war.) "The Union must & shall be preserved" says the robber who presents his carbine at your head & demands your watch, fine jewelry ... "This Union shall be preserved" says the ruffian who breaks your furniture, rips open your bedding, & then fires your house. The widespread desolation which Sherman caused in his march from Atlanta to Savannah & from thence to Columbia, was all done to preserve the Union—this glorious Union.

The people who inhabited the desolate region were no more considered than the chaff before the whirlwind. "The life of the nation must be preserved" says Seward no matter at what cost— even of the lives of this whole generation. To one who looks upon government as a means of ensuring life & property such language sounds like the ravings of insanity. But this insanity had evidently taken possession of the Northern & Western mind ... as was fearfully developed in the campaign of Sherman.

CHAPTER THREE

A SENATOR OFFERS PROOFS OF WAR CRIMES

IN MAY 1930, Senator Cole L. Blease of South Carolina delivered a speech in the United States Senate relating to the burning of Columbia and Sherman's culpability in that crime. Earlier, he had introduced bills to compensate some religious institutions in South Carolina for the damages caused by Sherman's army in 1865. The following excerpts are taken from Senator Blease's lengthy address to the Senate, which includes many sworn statements by eyewitnesses. The speech was published with the title *Destruction of Property in Columbia, S.C. by Sherman's Army.*

MR. BLEASE. That the city of Columbia, S.C., was burned in February, 1865, by Gen. W. T. Sherman's soldiers in accordance with and in satisfaction of what he expressed as "an insatiable desire to wreak vengeance upon South Carolina," and particularly upon her capital city, where the first secession convention met, and that the destruction of the city by fire was committed by his soldiers in his presence, with his knowledge, consent, acquiescence, and approval, is borne out by the truth of history, as will here be stated from the records.

The particular claims now pending are those of the Washington Street Methodist Episcopal Church and the Ladies' Ursuline Community. The church building of the former was set upon fire by Sherman's soldiers in the mistaken belief that it was the First Baptist Church nearby in which the secession convention had met. The convent of the Ladies' Ursuline Community was set upon fire by Sherman's soldiers that it might be looted of its rich treasures, which could not otherwise be done, because Sherman himself had personally promised its protection. The truth of these statements will be proved by facts which are incontrovertible. But there is a larger matter at issue. For 64 years there has been an effort to relieve Sherman and his army of the obloquy of this monstrous barbarity—an effort, coming from outside the South, first, to place the blame upon the Confederate general, Wade Hampton, and when the civilized world, and even the northern people, refused to give credence to a charge so incredible, then to make it appear an accident.

Edwin J. Scott, well known banker of unquestioned and unimpeachable integrity, then 62 years of age, and now long since gathered to his fathers, who was in Columbia, which was his home, that night, records in his diary which he kept an which he incorporated in his Random Recollections of a Long Life ... page181:

The Methodist Church on Washington Street was set on fire three times before its destruction was completed, Mr. Connor, the clergyman in charge, who lived in the parsonage adjoining, having twice put out the fire. When they burnt the parsonage he brought out a sick child wrapped in a blanket, and on one of the soldiers seizing the blanket he begged that it might be spared because of the child's sickness. The brute tore it off and threw it into the flames, saying, "D---n you, if you say a word I'll throw the child after it."

THE CONVENT OF THE LADIES' URSULINE COMMUNITY OF COLUMBIA

General Sherman personally promised protection to the convent. General Sherman admits this himself [in his memoirs] ...

Following is an excerpt from an affidavit given on April 6, 1928, by Mrs. H. W. Richardson, of Columbia, since deceased, a venerable and a venerated woman of a distinguished South Carolina family, who was a student in the convent at the time:

Soon thereafter the convent building was on fire and the occupants fled from the building. Upon leaving the building I saw soldiers of General Sherman's army on the roof of the convent building, and they were throwing firebrands and torches. Soon the buildings were in flames ...

THE SIGNAL ROCKETS AND THEN THE FIRES SET BY SHERMAN'S SOLDIERS

The testimony of numerous eyewitnesses is that the setting of numerous fires followed the signal rockets, most of them denominating them as "rockets"; but whether "rockets" or "fire balloons," the facts show that they were signals for the setting of the fires and the burning of Columbia ...

The following testimony was given before Sherman had retracted his charge that Columbia was burned by Hampton's men starting the general conflagration by burning cotton ... M. H. Berry, a northern man, whose sympathies were on the side of the Union, and who accompanied the Federal Army to the North when it left Columbia:

The first fire I saw, which was close to me, was set on fire by soldiers ... The place I saw set on fire was set on fire by soldiers wearing the uniform of United States soldiers ... General Hampton's troops left in the morning previous to the burning. They left fully four hours before I saw the cotton burning.

It has already been pointed out how the cotton was set on fire by Sherman's soldiers early in the day, shortly after they entered the city, and it is shown throughout the whole of all the narratives that this burning of cotton, though ignited by Sherman's soldiers, had nothing to do with the general conflagration that night.

Affidavit of W. B. Williams:

There was a good deal of cotton piled in the streets of the city prior to its occupation by the Federal forces ... but none was burned before the coming in of the Federal troops.

ADMISSION OF SHERMAN AND HIS OFFICERS

General Sherman did not, except momentarily, as it were, and then only by indirection, deny that his army burned Columbia. He charged it to General Hampton but soon withdrew that charge. Later, in his memoirs, he glossed it over as an accident, but he has never yet made specific denial of the fact, with the word "*accident*" (the italics being the italics of General Halleck, according to Sherman's Memoirs) staring him in the face, from General Halleck, Chief of Staff at Washington, that it was the kind of accident that was in contemplation. On the other hand, his high officers in Columbia at the time, have made the admission and given the facts.

That when he reached Columbia he saw an opportunity to burn Columbia, as he had already decided upon it before he left Atlanta, and charge the burning to Gen. Wade Hampton, of the

Confederate Army, and "distinctly" did so, and later, when the civilized world, and even the people of the North, could not be induced to accept so wild and reckless a charge, General Sherman "confessed" that he "did so pointedly to shake the faith of his— General Hampton's—people in him," according to General Sherman's own confession at a later date, the records show, and the witness who will be called upon this material point will be General Sherman himself:

In my official report of the conflagration (Sherman says in his Memoirs, written by himself) I distinctly charged it to Gen. Wade Hampton, and confess I did so pointedly, to shake the faith of his people in him, for he was, in my opinion, boastful and professed to be the special champion of South Carolina.

SHERMAN'S ACCIDENTS

In his Memoirs written by himself, Sherman says:

Many of the people thought that this fire was deliberately planned and executed. This is not true. It was an accident, and in my judgment began with the cotton which General Hampton's men had set fire to on leaving the city—

And so forth. When General Sherman wrote this in his Memoirs ... he himself had already abandoned the cotton theory. It might be well, however, here to emphasize the "*accident*" theory which seemed to pervade his then and later explanations. The words "*some accident*" constituted the keynote (for they were in italics, according to General Sherman) of the letter from Halleck to Sherman, under Washington date of December 18, 1864. The word "accident" lingered in the minds of the burners, and it was the word with which Sherman finally clothed the atrocity. His charge against General Hampton and Hampton's men he himself abandoned at the bar of public judgment.

GENERAL ADMISSIONS, INCLUDING SHERMAN'S

Neither in Columbia, nor afterwards, except when it came to the cold penning of it by himself for posterity, under his own name, whereof by himself he might be judged by posterity, did Sherman deny that his army burned Columbia. On the contrary, he admitted it. His only defense at the time was that it was inspired by liquor which his men found in Columbia ... He was a soldier who said that war was hell ... He was only a soldier and a disciplinarian and a general. He wrote much, including orders and including letters and reports to his superiors in military command. He never tried to explain or to make his conflicting statements coincide. He could not. He was on a mission which was ruthless, and ruthlessly he performed it. The South was stricken. Her armies were almost dissipated. There was practically no resistance in the path of Sherman's march. And yet he carried out a program which he must have formulated to be carried out in the face of stern military resistance.

When this program had been executed against a stricken people whose armies had been defeated and were then retreating to the final surrender, Sherman found it necessary, under the frowns of the civilized world and even of the people of the North, to explain and retract, and to excuse and to deny, and even to withdraw charges which he himself had made. His only reaction was to withdraw the charges against Hampton and his cavalry. His other statements remain conflicting.

THE VERDICT OF HISTORY

Percy Greg, English historian—History of the United States, by
Percy Greg, in two volumes, volume 2 ... pages 457 and 458—says:

On February 1, [1865], Sherman, with more than 60,000 men,
commenced his northward march through the Carolinas, a march
whose first and chief object was the ruin of the State which had
incurred the vindictive hatred of the northern people and
Government. He commenced the work of devastation as soon as
his army entered South Carolina ... Wade Hampton, who had been
detached to the rescue of his native State, and Wheeler were
unable to offer serious resistance, and Sherman without a battle
reached Columbia, the capital of the State, and one of the most
beautiful cities in the South. Wade Hampton denies that he burned
the cotton, to which the destruction of the city has been ascribed
by Sherman's apologists. His word is entitled to full confidence ...
After Sherman had entered the place a number of private houses
were fired and the city burned to ashes. From this disgrace he
strove to clear himself at Hampton's expense. It is certain that the
fires were lighted, and those who attempted to rescue their houses
were driven back by his soldiers with the sanction of their officers;
clear that Sherman made no attempt to restrain and no serious
effort to punish acts he afterwards thought it prudent to disown.
(Sherman expressly contradicts himself by saying that in his belief
the fire was accidental. The sufferers declare that Federal troops
prevented them from putting it out.

WHITELAW REID

The conclusion of the whole matter has been expressed by the Hon. Whitelaw Reid of Ohio on the war:

It was the most monstrous barbarity of this barbarous march. Before his movement began General Sherman begged permission to turn his army loose in South Carolina and devastate it. He used this permission to the full. He protested that he did not make war on women and children. But under the operation of his orders the last morsel of food was taken from hundreds of destitute families that his soldiers might feast in needless and riotous abundance. Before his eyes rose day after day the mournful clouds of smoke on every side that told of old people and their grandchildren driven in midwinter from the only roofs there were to shelter them by the flames which the wantonness of his soldiers had kindled. Yet if a single soldier was punished for a single outrage or theft during that entire movement we have found no mention of it in all the voluminous records of the march.

Narratives, statements, publications of various kinds have come from those who accompanied Sherman on that march. Search the records as one may, they contain either explanations or admissions. Nowhere is there a denial. All of them are apologetic. There is an underlying admission that the rules of civilized warfare had been suspended by Sherman or that there was a general understanding that these rules should not be enforced when Columbia was reached.

History shows that Sherman was a soldier of iron will, of determination which was stern and unyielding ... His letters to General Grant and General Halleck, and their letters to him, show that on this march he was supreme—that his was the judgment which governed.

But the South was stricken. The end was approaching, and none knew it better than General Halleck in Washington, and General Sherman before Savannah. From Atlanta Sherman's march was vengeance and not the stern necessity of war.

Sixty-four years is sufficient time for a proper perspective. With the destruction and desolation in his wake, carrying destruction and desolation as he went on from Columbia, it is inconceivable that an accident or the act of God should have coincided with his occupancy of Columbia to bring about the destruction of the city without the guiding hand and the flaming torches of his soldiers. Sufficient time has elapsed that sectional patriotism or prejudice, as one may choose to call it, should give way to the truth of history.

EXHIBITS

The following affidavits and documents are made a part of this record:

The Burning of the Ursuline Convent, Columbia, S.C., By Sherman's Army in 1865. An abridged copy, taken from the annals of the convent, written by a member of the community who was an eyewitness.

On February 17, 1865, General Sherman's army entered Columbia. Reverend Dr. O'Connell, pastor of St. Peter's Church and chaplain to the Ursulines asked a guard of protection for the convent. He obtained it—one man. On February 17, about noon, a cavalry officer rode up to the convent, spoke to the guard, and rang for admittance. Of the portress he asked to see the mother superioress. To the superioress, Mother Baptista Lynch, he introduced himself as Major Fitzgibbons, a Catholic, and offered any service he, as an individual, could render. The reverend mother, not suspecting any danger to the convent, declined, at the same time thanking him for the offer. He, earnestly insisting, said: "Columbia is a doomed city; at least, that is the talk of the Army; and I do not know if a house will be left standing."

Such an announcement startled the superioress; yet she and her companion answered that such threats could not apply to the convent, since General Sherman had given a patron of the institution the assurance that her daughter, a pupil, was in a place of safety.

The nuns could not be convinced that danger was imminent. Finally the major persuaded mother superior to write to the general, stating all the reasons she had given for her confidence of protection. He offered to be the bearer of the letter and said he would place it in the general's hand. The letter was written and intrusted to the major. About 3 o'clock that afternoon Major Fitzgibbons returned, accompanied by seven soldiers, whom he stated to be picked men sent to guard the convent. He also gave to mother superior the envelope which had inclosed her letter to the general, and on it Sherman had penciled orders to nearest commanding officer to protect the convent.

Scarcely had the nuns given supper to the seven guardsmen and gathered in the "community room" for the evening when the alarm of fire was given. From the windows the nuns saw the city toward the south blazing. Calling one of the guards, they asked him to go for Major Fitzgibbons. He refused. Other guards refused other services. The nuns saw that no assistance was to be expected from them.

Reverend Father McNeal called to remove the blessed sacrament. The suppressed sobs of the younger sisters but feebly expressed the deep emotion that filled all hearts.

Parents came running for their children, yet knew not where to take them for safety. The danger became so imminent and the crowds of soldiers so great that the pupils and the younger sisters were given bundles of clothing and marshaled into line as for a promenade. At a signal given by mother superior they marched quietly out. Reverend Father O'Connell accompanied them to the Catholic Church—the wind being from that direction, the edifice was deemed safe.

About midnight, by the light of the fast approaching flames, the plundering of the convent began. Heavy flakes of fire were falling over the premises. The nuns who had remained were admonished to leave. Reverend Doctor O'Connell wished to lead the nuns down Main street, but the flames were lashing one another from building to building. As the sisters stood bewildered, not knowing their own city, a gentleman on horseback called, "Follow me, sisters; I will lead you to safety." As they followed, flakes fell so fast on and about them that holes were burned in their veils and cloaks. In a short while, however, they were with their sisters in the churchyard.

MR. WHILDEN REPLIES TO HITCHCOCK'S STORY— COLUMBIAN WHO REMEMBERS THE BURNING OF COLUMBIA AND OCCUPATION OF CITY BY SHERMAN'S ARMY ANSWERS CHARGES MADE BY NORTHERN SOLDIER

In compliance with a number of requests, knowing that I am conversant with the actual facts, [I have] consented to reply to the review of Marching with Sherman, by Maj. Henry Hitchcock, which was published in the issue of The State of April 14, 1929.

An error is more dangerous to proportion to the degree of truth. It contains, and there is a sort of half-truth in some of Major Hitchcock's statements which give the evidence that he was here at that eventful time, but he is lacking in the accuracy of his statements ...

He writes: "We have now marched a great army diagonally and through the very heart of the first and most bitter and obstinate of all rebel States, without a single check, defeat, or disaster ... sweeping everything before us, consuming their substance, burning their cotton, etc."

However, he makes a valuable statement in "his diary" when he writes: "The really important things we have done are in the capture and destruction of Columbia and the railroads near it, the destruction of immense quantities of machinery, ammunition, ordnance, and military stores of all kinds." Does anyone want a stronger testimony of the fact that Sherman's army destroyed Columbia than this statement by one of his own officers?

"One more word about Columbia. It was not burned by orders but expressly against orders and in spite of the utmost efforts on our part to save it."

I do not propose to cite all or even a small part of the vast documentary evidence which fixes the guilt on General Sherman and his army, but I wish to record a personal reminiscence.

That evening two officers stepped upon the piazza and requested my mother to give them supper. This request mother complied with. Those two men were Capt. James G. Crosier, Twenty-first Illinois Regiment, and his lieutenant. (We have corresponded with Captain Crosier since the war; he retired as major.) After supper we all gathered about the fire and talked. About 8 o'clock they got up to go; they thanked mother for her hospitality, and as they were leaving Captain Crosier handed mother a bottle of glycerin, some licorice, and some medicine, with the remark: "You will have need of these before morning, as we have orders to destroy the city."

Our house on Laurel Street was set on fire by soldiers in the rear, when we were forced to leave. Remember, Major Hitchcock says in his diary: "The important things we have done are the capture and destruction of Columbia, S.C., etc."

I give you these evidences of fact. You may be the judge by the outcome of the truth of the statement.

At 8 p. m. three rockets were sent up from the statehouse; within an hour after the signal, which our whole family saw from our south piazza, fires were flaming up in all quarters of the city. This could not have been an accident or set by cotton flying about, nor by General Hampton or his faithful 400, because they had been out of the city at least 10 hours.

Again I quote [Hitchcock]:

"The streets were full of loose cotton brought out and set fire to by the rebels before they left. I saw it when we rode into town."

Now, what are the facts? Here again we have a half truth. In the lower part of the city cotton was brought from the warehouses into the streets to be destroyed or to prevent it falling into the hands of the enemy, but up to the time of the entering in of the army not a fire had been set nor a bale of cotton burned. It is now known that Hampton at the last minute gave orders for it not to be burned ...

The cotton bales were strapped by ropes; these bands were cut by the swords and bayonets of the Federal soldiers and scattered broadcast on the wings of the northwest gale that was blowing at the time, and soon the trees, streets, and parks were filled with loose cotton.

Sherman's army began to enter the city between 9 and 10 a. m. and marched down Main Street from what is now known as the Broad River Road, and they were marching in nearly all day. I was on Main Street and saw them come in. Major Hitchcock may have been among the number that came in late in the day, and the soldiers may have fired some cotton down by the railroad, but I did not see it, nor did I know of it.

A detachment of Sherman's army crossed the Congaree River at the foot of Bridge (now Gervais) Street on their own pontoon bridge and did not enter the city until late in the afternoon. Major Hitchcock may have been with this division, and his statement may have been correct, for the cotton on Bridge Street may have been fired before dark.

Gen. Wade Hampton made an orderly retreat from our city with his troops, about 400 in number, and passed our house on Laurel Street just before the head of Sherman's army marched into the city. I saw them go out ...

Up to this time they left not a fire was burning in the city, to my knowledge, nor was there any loose cotton flying about.

The first fire was seen after the entrance of the United States Army. They opened the jail and released the prisoners and then set fire to the building. This was about noon.

When the negro firemen carried the engines to the fire the soldiers drove the firemen away and with axes broke up the engines and with swords and bayonets cut the hose, rendering the outfit useless.

Now, all this can certainly not be laid to the door of General Hampton or his troops.

Once again I quote:

"The citizens themselves, like idiots, madmen, brought out large quantities of liquor as soon as our troops entered and distributed freely among them."

This charge I claim is absolutely false. My mother, grandmother, two servants, and the writer were on Main Street when the army was coming in and saw the stores broken open and entered by the army and liquor flowed freely from buckets in the hands of the United States soldiers ...

In the afternoon the city was crowded in every part with drunken soldiers, and they were very riotous.

A soldier, too drunk to protect himself, was burned to death on the steps of the back piazza of our home on Laurel Street.

It has been estimated (I understand) that hundreds of United States soldiers were burned to death entering homes uninvited and going to bed in the bedrooms of homes too drunk to arouse or protect themselves when the house was set on fire and burned to the ground with its contents. I am in a position to cite one instance.

It was "common talk" that when General Sherman became aware of this phase of the tragedy, about 2 a. m., he gave orders that the fires be stopped, and in an hour the flames were out. The fires did cease quite suddenly toward morning ...

I have only presented facts as I know them, for I was here and am thoroughly conversant with what I am writing about.

The more this matter is ventilated by the "northern side of the story," the more the evidence is produced that our beautiful capital city was destroyed deliberately and premeditatedly by General Sherman's army; and the truth may as well be admitted.

FRANK F. WHILDEN

CHAPTER FOUR

WADE HAMPTON MAKES HIS CASE

W ADE HAMPTON (1818-1902), a wealthy South Carolina planter, was a beloved hero to the people of his state during and after the war. He entered Confederate military service as a private but soon raised a unit of infantry, artillery and cavalry known as Hampton Legion. He was a successful officer and was frequently selected for detached service. In 1864 became the commander of Gen. Robert E. Lee's cavalry, and his final post was the command of Gen. Joseph E. Johnston's cavalry. General Hampton was outraged when he learned that General Sherman had falsely accused him of causing the fire that destroyed the capital city of his native state. In reaction to proceedings of a "mixed commission" appointed to investigate and adjudicate war claims by British and American citizens, he wrote a lengthy response which was first published in the *Baltimore Enquirer* newspaper on June 24, 1873. In 1888, it was reprinted in a pamphlet published by Walker, Evans & Cogswell.

BURNING COLUMBIA "THE MOST MONSTROUS BARBARITY OF A BARBAROUS MARCH"

Wade Hampton's Presentation of the Case—The Testimony of Sherman and his Officers—Guilt Fixed Beyond Evasion or Recall—The Whole Infamous Story Completely Told—Sherman's Army Convicted of the Crime

A "mixed commission on American and British claims" is now holding its sessions in Washington, and before this tribunal will soon be brought cases involving the question of the destruction of Columbia, S.C., in February, 1865. With these cases I am in no wise connected, nor am I otherwise interested, save in showing the truth of the matter, and thus relieving myself from the false charge which has associated my name with this great outrage.

In order to establish these points beyond all question, it will be necessary to discuss the matter at some length, and to submit a large mass of documentary evidence. Let me, therefore, crave in advance the indulgence of your readers, hoping that their interest in seeing the truth of history vindicated will give them patience to consider and weigh the evidence advanced. This controversy has been forced upon me for the second time, by Gen. W. T. Sherman's reckless disregard of truth in his assaults upon me, before this "mixed commission;" and if the testimony which will be produced shall prove how utterly unworthy of credit his assertions are, he will have no one to blame except himself. He shall be dealt with in the manner that all defamers deserve, and my language shall be so plain and the proofs so overwhelming that even he himself can understand, obtuse though he may be to the obligations due to or from a gentleman.

On the night of the 17th February, 1865, Columbia was burned to the ground after it had been in the possession of the Federal troops for ten hours. How was it so burned? No one of the citizens who was present during that disastrous night would be at a moment's loss to answer that question, and many of them have answered it most conclusively, as will be shown in the course of this narrative. No one there doubted or doubts to whom the guilt attaches, and it was with surprise and indignation that my fellow-citizens saw the charge in Sherman's official report, published in

April, 1865, that the destruction had been caused by myself. In this report the following language is used:

SHERMAN'S WANTON STATEMENTS

"Gen. Wade Hampton, who commanded the Confederate rear-guard of cavalry, had, in anticipation of our capture of Columbia, ordered that all the cotton, public and private, should be moved into the streets and fired to prevent our making use of it ... Some of these piles of cotton were burning," (when the Federal troops entered the city) "especially in the heart of the city, near the Courthouse, but the fire was partially subdued by the labor of our soldiers ... Before one single public building had been fired by order, the smouldering fires, set by Hampton's order, were rekindled by the wind and communicated to the buildings around. I disclaim on the part of my army any agency in this fire, but on the contrary claim that we saved what of Columbia remains unconsumed. And without hesitation I charge Gen. Wade Hampton with having burned his own city of Columbia, not with malicious intent, or as the manifestation of a silly 'Roman stoicism,' but from folly and want of sense, in filling it with lint cotton and tinder."

This was the insulting charge first made by Sherman, and made in the most offensive terms, at a time when I was a prisoner of war, under parole, and thus unable to meet it in the only manner it deserved. But one mode of answering was open to me, and the one least agreeable to my wishes, that of denouncing it as false in the public prints, and this was done on the 19th June, 1865, in the following terms:

"It would be difficult, if not impossible, to express in an equal number of paragraphs, a greater number of falsehoods than are contained in the above extracts. There is not one word of truth in

41

all that has been quoted, except the statement that 'Gen. Hampton commanded the rear-guard of the cavalry.' He did not order any cotton 'moved into the streets and fired.' On the contrary, my first act on taking command of the cavalry, to which I was assigned only the night before the evacuation of Columbia, was to represent to Gen. Beauregard the dangers to the town of firing the cotton in the streets. Upon this representation he authorized me to give orders that no cotton in the town should be fired, which orders were strictly carried out. I left the city after the head of Sherman's column entered it, and I assert what can be proved by thousands, that not one bale of cotton was on fire when he took possession of the city. His assertion to the contrary is false, and he knows it to be so."

These extracts from my letter will be sufficient to show how the charge made by Sherman was met ... This was all I could do, for I was debarred by my position from seeking the proper redress for this wanton insult of Gen. Sherman, which never would have been given had I been free to resent it as it deserved ... Fortunately for the people of the South, reunion and reconstruction, if they have brought in their train no other privileges, have at least restored to every man the right to resent an insult and to brand a falsehood from whatever quarter they may come; and in the exercise of this only right that is restored, I now feel at liberty to discuss the questions at issue on terms of equality with Gen. Sherman. In doing this I shall submit unimpeachable evidence to show the charge made against me by Sherman is utterly false, and also that his own men burned Columbia after he had promised protection to property and citizens ...

While serving on the staff of Gen. Beauregard he directed me to issue an order that all cotton stored in Columbia should be placed where it could burned, "in case of necessity, without danger of destroying buildings." This order was published in one of the city papers on the 15th February, I think, and is doubtless the same to which Sherman alludes in one of his numerous communications relative to the destruction of Columbia—an allusion which will be noticed in the proper place. The post commander of Columbia at that time was Major Allen J. Green, a gallant officer and a gentleman of the highest character. He has been kind enough to send me the following paper, which speaks for itself:

NO ORDER TO BURN THE COTTON

Huntsville, Ala. December 31, 1872

Having been requested to give my recollections of the events connected with the evacuation of Columbia, South Carolina, on the 17th of February, 1865, I would state that at the time of said evacuation by the Confederate forces I was post commander of that city. That a day or two before the evacuation I received an order from Lieut. Gen. Wade Hampton, directing me to ascertain what amount of cotton there might be in the city ... and to remove the same to the vacant fields or lots adjacent, in order not to endanger the town should the necessity arise for burning the same; that not having sufficient transportation at my command to execute Hampton's order, I directed such cotton as had not already been removed to be placed in a narrow line along the centre of Main or Richardson street, that the citizens themselves might be able to watch it and thus prevent a general conflagration, should a subsequent order be given to burn it; that no such order to burn it was ever received by me, but that either during the night previous to or on the day of the evacuation, a second order was received by me from Gen. Hampton, directing me to take no further steps with regard to the cotton, as it was not deemed necessary to destroy it. And I would further state that being in charge of the post, with my immediate command on duty up to the last moment of the evacuation, (which was between 10 and 11 o'clock A.M., to the best of my recollection) no fires had occurred in the city up to that time, and to the best of my knowledge and belief no cotton or other material had been set on fire by any orders from Gen. Hampton, nor by any troops under his command.

ALLEN J. GREEN

This affidavit of Major Green shows how and why the cotton was placed in the streets, and it proves how utterly unfounded is the assertion of Sherman, that I "had ordered all the cotton should be moved into the streets and fired."

THE ORDERS NOT TO BURN

CHARLESTON, August 13, 1866

[To:] Chancellor J. P. Carroll, Chairman of the Committee for the Investigation of the Burning of Columbia

Sir: Seeing that you have called for a testimony in reference to the destruction of Columbia by fire ... I beg to make the following statement: Soon after Gen. Hampton assumed command of the cavalry, which he did on the morning of 17th February, he told me that Gen. Beauregard had determined not to burn the cotton, as the Yankees had destroyed the railroad, and he directed me to issue an order that no cotton be fired. This I did at once, and when I left Columbia, which I did after the entrance of the Federal troops, not one bale of cotton was burning, nor had one been fired by our troops. At the time referred to I was acting as A. A.[Assistant Adjutant] General to Gen. Hampton.

Very respectfully, your obedient servant,

Rawlins Lowndes, Captain and A. A. G.

SOME INTERESTING EVIDENCE

Though the proofs adduced are sufficient to convince every impartial mind that orders were issued not to burn the cotton, I shall add one more. On the 22nd April, 1866, I wrote to Gen. Beauregard in reference to this matter ...

NEW ORLEANS, May 2, 1866

The above statement of Gen. Hampton relative to the order issued by me at Columbia, South Carolina, not to burn the cotton in that city, is perfectly true and correct. The only thing on fire at the time of the evacuation was the depot building of the South Carolina Railroad, which caught fire accidentally from the explosion of some ammunition ordered to be sent toward Charlotte, N.C.

G. T. Beauregard

It may be mentioned here that this depot was an isolated building near the river and distant from the business portion of the city about one mile. Reference will be made to its destruction in another place.

It will scarcely be necessary to present any further evidence to show that no cotton was fired by my order. So we may turn to the next sentence of the official report of Sherman, which has been quoted: "Some of these piles of cotton were burning" ... To meet this assertion the following papers are given.

FEDERAL SOLDIERS KINDLE THE FLAMES AND CUT THE ENGINE HOSE

"Mich. H. Berry, being sworn, deposed: 'I was in Columbia in February, 1865, when the city was burned ... The first fire I saw, which was close to me, was set on fire by soldiers ... After the army came in, about 12 o'clock, I came down the street to the old market on Main street. There was cotton in the street near the Courthouse; the wind commenced blowing a lively breeze, and the cotton took fire ... The citizens and soldiers ran out the hose carriage and put the fire out ... Gen. Hampton's troops left in the morning previous to the burning. They left fully four hours before I saw the cotton burning as stated.'"

Now, here is a witness who swears that our troops had left four hours before he saw the cotton burning, and that it was not burning when he first saw it ...

The next deposition is that of Orlando Z. Bates, an alderman of the city: "In company with the mayor, Hon. T. J. Goodwyn, and Aldermen McKenzie and Stork, I proceeded to the outskirts of the city and met the advance guard of the Federal army, under command of Col. Stone ... [I] returned to the city about 12 or 1 o'clock ... There was no alarm of fire, and no burning of any description previous to the occupation already stated. The conflagration commenced after the entry of the United States forces. I saw the burning of several houses ... I was present with the fire company aiding to extinguish it, and saw Federal soldiers sticking bayonets into the engine hose, and cutting the same with hatchets and knives ... I will also state that a quantity of cotton had been brought out of the cellars of stores, ... piled in the middle of street. As the troops passed it *I saw the cotton fired by them, striking matches and applying* ... I saw several instances of Federal soldiers actually applying fire to buildings, and others carrying torches to various parts of the city for the same purpose." (The italics are mine.)

James G. Gibbes, who was subsequently mayor of the city, testifies: "An alarm of fire arose, caused by the burning of some cotton in Richardson street. It was set on fire by the United States soldiers ... The United States soldiers began to riddle and cut up the hose with their bayonets ... About 7 o'clock in the evening three or four rockets were thrown up in the extreme northwestern portion of the city ... I saw various of the soldiers with bottles with some inflammable material—I supposed it to be turpentine—with which they made fire-balls and started fire in the buildings that way. My father's house was burned by them after having escaped the general conflagration. It was a fire-proof building and had escaped the flames. I saw them fire furniture in the house, turn over the piano, tables, chairs, and starting the fire from lace curtains, &c, &c."

WITH THE CONSENT OF THEIR OFFICERS

The whole testimony given by this witness, and by the last, is valuable, but it is too long to be inserted here. All, however, will go before the mixed commission.

Joseph Samson swears: "I saw colonels and captains with their soldiers while they were pillaging; and I saw no effort made by them to put a stop to these acts."

John A. Civil swears: "I saw United States soldiers, officers being present with them, put fire to houses."

"South Carolina, Chester District: Personally appeared before me this 24th day of May, 1866, William Thompson, citizen of the State and district aforesaid, and swore that he was a resident of

Columbia during February, 1865, witnessed the entry of the United States forces under Gen. Sherman, and that there was no fire in the city at or before that time ... Deponent was a fireman, and together with other firemen endeavored to check and extinguish the flames, but the hose of their engine was cut and pierced by axes, bayonets and other instruments in the hands of the Federal soldiers ... Deponent further stated that his house was burned by two Federal soldiers, who repeatedly said, 'The d-----d town ought to be burned,' and that it was always their intention to burn it.   WM. THOMPSON

"Sworn to before me this 24th day of May, 1866.   GILES G. PATTERSON."

In addition to the proofs already given ... I add the following ... The first paper submitted is the affidavit of the mayor of Columbia ... He speaks of what he saw and was cognizant of, and I ask special attention to his declarations:

MAYOR GOODWYN'S TESTIMONY

Two or three days previous to the surrender of the city of Columbia, it was under martial law ... On the 16th of February, 1865, the enemy appeared on the Lexington side of the river, and early in the day commenced shelling the city and continued until night without ever demanding a surrender, all our women and children and aged citizens exposed to their fire ... On the morning of the 17th at day dawn there was an explosion at the Charleston depot (from accident) that aroused everyone. I was summoned to the Town Hall in order to prepare for surrendering the city. In consulting with several aldermen, we determined to raise the white flag over the market steeple. Whilst preparing to do so, Gen. Hampton sent me word not to do so until he gave me further orders. Between 8 and 9 o'clock he rode up and said that I now could proceed. Whilst sitting on his horse he observed some cotton piled not far off in the middle of the street. He advised me to put a guard over it, saying some careless ones by smoking might set it afire, and in so doing would endanger the city. From that hour I saw nothing more of Gen. Hampton until the war was over, and have every reason to believe that he left the city very soon afterwards. In company with three of the aldermen, viz: Messrs McKenzie, Bates and Stork, I went in a carriage with a white flag and met the enemy near Broad River. The first general officer we met was Col. Stone, (acting brigadier;) he accepted the surrender, and said he would proceed with us and take possession, guaranteeing protection until Gen. Sherman arrived. I requested him to send a letter to the general ...

I was compelled to be most of my time from home, and my house was completely stripped before the fire. The first time I saw Gen. Sherman was between two and three o'clock in the evening, nearly opposite the town hall. I went out and spoke to him. He said he had received my letter, and that it would be all right; asked me for a house, to which I sent a servant with him. He asked me to come round in the course of the evening to see him. I went round very soon afterwards; found him very polite and courteous, promising protection to our city. He got me to take a walk with him, and introduced to him a new and old acquaintance. On our return about sundown when parting he said, "Go home and rest assured that your city will be as secure in my hands as if you had control!" He then stopped me and asked the condition of our fire engine and water-works. I replied that they were all in good order; said he was pleased to hear it, for he was compelled to burn some of the public buildings, and in doing so he did not wish to destroy one particle of private property; this evening, he said, was too windy to do anything. On my arrival home about dusk, three rockets went up in front of my house—red, blue and white. At that time there was a very quiet and good soldier sitting in my piazza;

he jumped up, and exclaimed, "My God, is it coming to this!" My wife asked him what he meant; he made no reply and walked off. In fifteen minutes afterwards there was a cry of fire on Main street, near Janney's. I went there and worked some time, until I was informed that the city was being set on fire in many places by soldiers with torches. Our engines were broken and our hose cut, and our city by 8 o'clock in ashes. I saw very few drunken soldiers that night. Many sober soldiers, that appeared to sympathize with our people, told me that the fate and doom of Columbia was common talk around their camp fires ever since they left Savannah. The next morning I was suffering very much from an inflamed eye caused by a spark of fire. That night Gen. Sherman sent for me. I went to see him about 1 o'clock. He met me very cordially, and said that he regretted very much that our city was burnt, and that it was my fault. I asked him how? He said, "In suffering ardent spirits to be left in the city after it was evacuated," saying: "Who could command drunken soldiers?" There was no allusion made to Gen. Hampton, no accident, or to cotton. It is perfectly absurd in charging Gen. Hampton with the burning of Columbia. Every man living in the city was his admirer and friend, and he knew it would impoverish them and their children, and bring us all near to starvation and ruin. The soldiers of Gen. Sherman's army burnt Columbia.   T. J. GOODWYN

PREMEDITATED DESTRUCTION

The first paper to which attention is asked is the affidavit of Edwin J. Scott, one of the most prominent and worthy citizens of Columbia. As his statement is too long to be inserted entire, extracts are taken from it. I regret that space cannot be found for the whole of it:

I asked Col. Stone whether private property would be respected in the city. He replied in these words: "Private property will be respected. We are not savages. If you let us alone, we will let you alone." He looked and spoke like a gentleman, and I believed him. Others in my hearing received the same assurances ... I neither saw any fire nor heard any alarm when at Main street, though there were crowds of soldiers and citizens in every direction, and I passed within two hundred feet of the cotton ... I met Col. Stone, whose word had been so solemnly pledged for the protection of property in the morning. To him I stated that a large number of boxes, trunks and packages, belonging to private individuals, and containing property and papers of great value, were in the vaults of the bank, while the apartments overhead and in the rear were occupied by women and children, with their furniture, food, clothes, &c, for which I begged that a guard might be sent. But though standing idle in the crowd, he turned me off, with the remark that he had no time to attend to me. The street was by this time so thronged with drunken and disorderly soldiers that it seemed impossible to get through them, and I proceded around the square to reach Nicholson's Hotel, where Major Jenkins, the provost marshal, was said to be quartered. I found that officer surrounded by many of our citizens, and some ladies, all anxiously seeking protection. As soon as his attention could be gained, I made a hasty statement of the condition of things at the bank, and appealed to him for a guard for the family and the property. His answer was, "I cannot undertake to protect private property." ...

There certainly was no fire at sunset and for some time previous when these scenes were enacting in that part of the street where the cotton was burning in the forenoon for it contained more men than I have ever seen in the same space, either before or since; yet there was no alarm or appearance of fire ... But for a change of wind just before day, all that portion of the city where I reside would have been destroyed ... At Col. Duncan's house we were introduced to Gen. Sherman. He referred to the burning of the city, admitting that it was done by his troops, but excusing them because, as he alleged, they had been made drunk by our citizens ... He never mentioned or alluded in any way to Gen. Hampton or the cotton, nor gave the slightest intimation that they were instrumental in the destruction of the city ... At that time the universal testimony of our people was that Sherman's troops burnt the place, and although they left here loaded with plunder from the houses they had destroyed, not one of them, so far as I have ever heard, was punished, tried, arrested, or even questioned for his conduct whilst in this city. Since then I have been in daily intercourse with all classes in and about Columbia, high and low, rich and poor, male and female, white and black; yet I have not met with a single person who attributed this calamity to any other cause. If a transaction that occurred in the presence of forty or fifty thousand people can be successfully falsified, then all human evidence is worthless and all history may be regarded as a collection of fables.

OFFICERS AND SOLDIERS APPLYING THEIR TORCHES

I present now the deposition of Rowland Keenan, another old and worthy citizen: "I am a resident of Columbia, and was present at the burning of Columbia on the 17th of February, 1865. I saw, during that burning, soldiers in the uniform of the United States setting fire to buildings in Cotton Town. At that time there were

United States officers mingling in the crowd, and they made no effort to prevent the burning."

Charles F. Jackson swears: "I was on Main street in the city of Columbia on the occasion of the entry of the main army of Gen. Sherman on the 17th of February, 1865. On the night following I witnessed United States soldiers with balls of combustible material, lighting them and flinging them about the streets and over and under the houses, Federal officers at the same time mingling with the crowd. I saw a United States officer, who stated to me that the burning of Columbia was premeditated. He further stated that any statement made by Gen. Sherman to the contrary was a lie."

I ask now to give the affidavit of Mrs. Agnes Law, which, from its directness, its simplicity and its pathos must command credence:

State of South Carolina, Richland District: "I am now seventy-two years old. I have lived in this town forty-eight years. My dwelling-house was at the corner of Main and Laurel streets, a brick house, three stories, slate roof, with large gardens on two sides. When Columbia was burnt, my sister, Mrs. Jane Scott, was with me; also a niece of mine, recently confined [that is, late pregnancy], who had not yet ventured out of the house. When Gen. Sherman took possession, I got four guards. They were well behaved and sober men. I gave them supper. One lay down on the sofa, and the other walked about. When the city began to burn, I wished to move my furniture out. They objected; said my house was in no danger, it was fire-proof. I insisted on moving out, but one replied, 'If I were as safe till the end of the war as this house is from fire, I would be satisfied.' Not long afterwards these guards themselves took lighted candles from the mantelpiece and went upstairs. At the same time other soldiers crowded into the house.

My sister followed them up-stairs, but came down very soon to say, 'They are setting the curtains on fire.' Soon the whole house was in a blaze. Some of the soldiers put boxes of matches under the bookcase in the parlor. Some put these boxes into wheat straw which I had under my back store. When those who had set fire up-stairs came down, they said to me, 'Old woman, if you don't want to burn up with your house, you'd better get out of it!' My niece had been carried to the Taylor House on Arsenal Hill. I went to the door to see if I could get any person I knew to assist me up there. I had been very sick, and liable to convulsions, and I could not walk alone. I could see no friend—only crowds of Federal soldiers. I was afraid I should fall on the street and be burnt up in the flames of the houses blazing on both sides of the streets. I had to go alone. I spent that night at the Taylor House, which a Federal officer said should not be burned, out of pity for my niece. The next two nights I passed in my garden without any shelter. Nothing was saved out of my house but one chair, two mattresses and one large looking-glass. I have been over fifty years a member of the Presbyterian Church. I cannot live long. I shall meet Gen. Sherman and his soldiers at the bar of God. I give this testimony against them in full view of that dread tribunal. AGNES LAW."

THE TESTIMONY OF "LOYAL" WITNESSES

The first author from whom I quote is Capt. Conyngham, who accompanied the Federal army in its march through the South. Speaking of Columbia, he says: "As soon as night set in there ensued a sad scene indeed. The suburbs were first set on fire, some assert by the burning cotton which the Rebels had piled along the streets. Pillaging gangs soon fired the heart of the town, then entered houses, in many instances carrying off articles of value. I trust I shall never witness such a scene again—drunken soldiers rushing from house to house, emptying them of their valuables and then firing them ... Officers and men reveling on wines and liquors until the burning houses buried them in their drunken orgies."

Describing the scenes along the line of march, the same writer says: "If a house was empty this was prima facie evidence that the owners were Rebels, and all was sure to be consigned to the flames. If they remained at home it was taken for granted that everyone in South Carolina was a Rebel, and the chances were the place was consumed ... The ruined homesteads of the Palmetto State will long be remembered. The army might safely march the darkest night, the crackling pine woods shooting up their columns of flame, and the burning houses along the way would light it on ... I hazard nothing in saying that three-fifths in value of the personal property of the counties we passed through were taken by Sherman's army. The graves even were ransacked. The scenes I witnessed in Columbia were scenes that would have driven Alaric the Goth into frenzied ecstasies had he witnessed them."

This is pretty strong testimony to come from one who was a member of Gen. Sherman's military family, as I believe Capt. Conyngham to have been, and who thus had a full opportunity to witness the barbarous scenes he describes so graphically. Dismissing him, we will turn to Major Nichols, who was also on Sherman's staff, and hear what he has to say.

"The actual invasion of South Carolina has begun. The well-known sight of columns of black smoke meets our gaze again; this time houses are burning. Wherever our footsteps pass, fire, ashes and desolation fall in the path ... In the record of great wars we read of vast armies marching through an enemy's country, carrying death and destruction in their path; of villages burned, cities pillaged, a tribe or a nation swept out of existence. History, however, will be searched in vain for a parallel to the scattering and destructive effects of this invasion of the Carolinas. Cotton gins, presses, factories and mills were burned to the ground on every side: the head, centre and rear of our column might be traced by columns of smoke by day, and the glare of fires by night."

Rebel writers could scarcely draw a darker picture or a truer one of the horrors perpetrated by the Federal soldiery than is given by these members of Sherman's staff.

THE MOST MONSTROUS BARBARITY
OF A BARBAROUS MARCH

The following extract is taken from a work entitled "Ohio in the War," written by Whitelaw Reid, editor of the New York Tribune:

"When Sherman rode into Columbia piles of cotton which Wade Hampton had fired lay smouldering through the streets ... The soldiers extinguished the fires, as they supposed, but at nightfall they broke out again, doubtless in one or two places, from the burning cotton; but, as if by concert, there suddenly came cries of alarm from a dozen different quarters. The city was on fire in as many places ... Before morning a large portion of the city was in ruins. Thus helpless women and children were suddenly made homeless in an hour, in the night, in the winter. It was the most monstrous barbarity of the barbarous march. There is no reason to think that Gen. Sherman knew anything of the purpose to burn the city, which had been freely talked about among the soldiers through the afternoon; but there is reason to think that he knew well enough who did it, that he never rebuked it, and made no effort to punish it, except that he sought, indeed, to show that the enemy himself had burned his own city, not with malicious intent, but from folly and want of sense."

Yet in the same paragraph he admits everything, except the original starting of the first fire: "The officers and men not on duty, including the officers who had long been in prison there, may have assisted in spreading the fire after it once began, and may have indulged in unconcealed joy at seeing the ruin of the capital of South Carolina."

Much more of such comments could be taken from this book, but this is sufficient, and with this I close the extracts from Northern sources, though the field is ample. There is, however, one affidavit which should be placed on the record as it may have peculiar weight with our Northern brethren. It is that of William Beverly Nash, colored State Senator, member of the convention which nominated Gen. Grant for the Presidency, and a leader of the great Republican party. The paper is as follows:

"State of South Carolina, Richland District: Personally appeared before me W. B. Nash, who, being duly sworn, says that he never made an affidavit in relation to the burning of Columbia; that he made a statement of the blowing up the depot by accident, and that a few bales of cotton were burned by private parties, to an officer connected with the Freedmen's Bureau. Deponent further states that Gen. Sherman, or men acting under his permission, burned the city of Columbia, and that Gen. Hampton had nothing to do with the nefarious transaction. W.B. NASH.

"Sworn to before me this 21st day of May, A. D. 1866. W. B. JOHNSTON, Magistrate."

Besides the evidence adduced to show by whom Columbia was burned, much can be brought forward to prove that the destruction of the city was premeditated. Indeed, there is very strong reason to suppose that Sherman himself, in spite of his solemn declarations to the contrary, had not only determined to destroy the city, but had expressed this determination. Certain it is that the fate of the place was discussed openly among his men long before its capture, and its destruction predicted. The first paper bearing on this point to be submitted is the affidavit of R. Speer, which is subjoined:

SHERMAN'S INTENTIONS—
"COLUMBIA SHALL BE BURNT"

"Georgia, Bartow County: Personally appeared before me came Robert Speer, of said county and State, who being sworn, deposes and says he is a citizen of said county and State, and resides near Eufaula, about sixty miles from Atlanta; that he was a citizen of said county and State at the time that Gen. W. T. Sherman made his raid through Georgia, and was taken a prisoner by Col. Wilder, of Gen. Sherman's command, and taken to his, the said Sherman's, headquarters at Kingston, Ga., and was severely catechized by the said Sherman. During the conversation had with him at his headquarters Gen. Sherman distinctly stated and avowed that the destruction of with which he was then visiting the citizens of Georgia, would be nothing to compare with what he had in store for the State of South Carolina; that looking upon her as an aggressor, that he would 'grease that State over and burn it up,' that 'he would have her people howling after me (Gen. Sherman) for bread.' 'All he wanted was guns and men, and damned if he did not have them.' This statement can be abundantly corroborated by other witnesses. R. SPEER.

"Sworn and subscribed to before me this the 12th day of October, A. D., 1868. J. A. A. BLACKBURN, Attorney at Law."

This is rather an ugly record for Gen. Sherman, and unfortunately for him there are other others of the same kind. The following extracts are taken from depositions which are to go before the mixed commission:

"Mr. John R. Niernsee, the architect who designed the State House in Columbia, testifies as follows: "I was a resident of Columbia on the 17th of February, 1865, and on the evening of that day I met Capt. Ritner of the 77th Illinois regiment. I saw rockets going up and asked him the meaning of it. He drew me aside, so my wife could not hear it, and said 'Major, this is the signal for the burning of your city.' The brigade that set fire to the town marched past my house with the implements in their possession for setting fire."

Mrs. Rachel Susan Cheves, widow of the late John R. Cheves, testifies as follows: "I resided in Savannah, Georgia, at the time of the occupation of said city by the forces of the United States under Gen. Sherman in the winter of 1864 and 1865. I was warned by two officers of Gen. Sherman's staff, Col. Poe and Major Dayton, not to go to Columbia, as they intended to burn it. I think his words were that they would pass through South Carolina with the torch as well as the sword. These officers were quartered with me. I had asked to be passed through the lines in a flag of truce boat. They warned me as an act of kindness not to go, as they intended to burn every town through which they passed in South Carolina. I told them I intended to go to Columbia, and they said I had better stay where I was, as Sherman intended to burn Columbia."

This testimony is corroborated by that of Mrs. Langdon Cheves, who was present when the conversation referred to took place.

Mrs. Anna W. Barclay, the wife of the late British consul at New York, testifies that she was at the house of Miss Telfair, in Savannah, in December, 1864, and heard Gen. Sherman in a conversation refer to the city of Columbia. He remarked that his course through Georgia had been marked by fire, and that through South Carolina it should be marked by fire and blood, and in his own words: "As to that hotbed of secession, Columbia, I shall lay it in ashes." Upon the expression of horror and regret of some person present, he repeated his assertion, "Columbia shall be burnt."

Mr. William H. Orchard, of Columbia, testified that on the night of the 17th of February a squad of Federal cavalry came up to his house, broke open his smoke house and took therefrom whatever they desired. "When they were leaving one of them turned back and said: 'You appear to have a large family here and you are a clever kind of man, let me give you a little advice; if you have anything to conceal, conceal it at once, for before morning this damned town will be in ashes.' My reply was: 'Is that so?' He said: 'Yes, and if you look out a little after dark you will see three rockets going up from the other side of the town, and if you have not taken my advice before then it will be too late.' I reported it to my wife, and we immediately set about saving a few things to escape with, and while engaged in doing so we observed the rockets, as was predicted, and within twenty minutes of that time I counted eight fires in different directions. I saw hundreds of Sherman's men setting fire to the town by means of camphine balls prepared for that purpose. There was a large box of them concealed in my yard early in the day. At night they took them out and made use of them. I saw them set fire to Phillip's auction-room and to my house. I attempted to put it out, but was knocked down by a Federal soldier, who told me I was a damned fool for making any such effort, and that my house was to be burned anyhow, and I had better save myself. There were a great many Federal officers of all grades on the streets mingling with the soldiers."

A HINT FROM HEADQUARTERS BORNE IN MIND

It appears to me that the charge of premeditated destruction of Columbia against Sherman and his men is as clearly sustained by the evidence as that of having burned the city, but as every link in the chain is important, one more may be added, which shall be taken from high official source, the record of the committee of Congress upon the conduct of the war. From this report the following extracts are made. The first is from a letter of Gen. Halleck, chief-of-staff in Washington, to Gen. Sherman: "Should you capture Charleston, I hope by some accident the place may be destroyed; and if a little salt should be thrown upon its site, it may prevent the growth of future crops of nullification or secession."

Was a more monstrous, cold-blooded, and barbarous order ever given, or given in a meaner way? "I hope that by some accident the place may be destroyed!" It fell upon willing and appreciative ears, for the reply is characterized by the same spirit that marks the order: "I will bear in mind," says Sherman, "your hint as to Charleston, and don't think salt will be necessary. When I move, the 15th corps will be on the right of the right wing, and their position will bring them naturally into Charleston first; and if you have watched the history of that corps, you will have remarked that they generally do their work up pretty well. The truth is, the whole army is burning with an insatiable desire to wreak vengeance on South Carolina. I almost tremble at her fate, but feel that she deserves all that seems in store for her. I look upon Columbia as quite as bad as Charleston."

If any reader is curious to follow up the history of the events which this correspondence foreshadows, I refer him to the "Conduct of the War," where he will find some singular and suggestive coincidences. One of the most remarkable is that the very last order issued by Sherman before the surrender of the city was to Howard to throw the 15th corps into Columbia, and another is that the town was destroyed while in the possession of that corps. They did, indeed, "do their work up pretty well." "Salt was not necessary." These were, indeed, strange coincidences—almost enough to make any impartial jury decide, if the question was left to them, that orders had been given from headquarters for the destruction of Columbia, and that the very instruments of its destruction had been designated. Any other incendiary would be convicted of arson on proof as strong as these letters and the events following them furnish.

SUPPRESSED REPORTS—A SIGNIFICANT SILENCE

Another significant fact in connection with those events deserving notice as having an important bearing in determining who is responsible for the burning of Columbia. In the "Conduct of the War" there will be found on almost every page of that portion relating to the march of Sherman through the Southern States letters, reports and dispatches from him, giving accounts of his movements and progress ... The order to Howard, to reference has already been made, is dated, if my memory serves me right, on the 16th of February, and the next communication from Sherman bears date, I think, on the 21st. Now how does it happen that so long an interval passed without any reports to headquarters in Washington? And stranger still, how is it that no reference at all is made to the capture and destruction of Columbia? Is this omission not passing strange? Can any sane man be persuaded that no mention was made by Sherman in his reports to Washington of the surrender and fate of the capital of South Carolina? To me it seems as though some letters have been suppressed because they told an ugly story of Columbia. If Sherman is as anxious as he appears to be to relieve himself from the odium attaching to the burning of that place, let him produce all his correspondence, or at least let him bring credible witnesses to prove that no letters have been withheld. Until he does this a grave suspicion must rest on him as being guilty not only of the suggestiofalsi, but of the suppressioveri.

Gen. Howard's name having been mentioned, reminds me of what had been nearly forgotten, that he is himself a most important witness in this case ... In December, 1866, or January, 1867, Gen. O. O. Howard came into the Executive office of Governor Orr, in Columbia, accompanied by Gen. R. K. Scott, and there found Governor Orr, Gen. John S. Preston, Mr. DeFontaine, the secretary of the Governor, and myself. In the course of the conversation that ensued the question of the burning of the city came up. Gen. Howard expressed sorrow as its destruction, and said that he had nothing to do with it, that he had done all he could to prevent it, and that he regretted it greatly. He then used the following language, which I committed to writing and left the paper with Dr. D. H. Trezevant, of Columbia, who had prepared for the press some articles relating to the destruction of the city. The memorandum is as follows:

GEN. O. O. HOWARD ON THE STAND

"Gen. O. O. Howard stated in the presence of Governor Orr, Gen. Preston and myself, that certainly no one was authorized to state that their (our) troops did not set fires in this town, for he himself saw them doing so. WADE HAMPTON"

This acknowledgment was so explicit, and as he was in command of the troops in the city, so conclusive, that I looked to his evidence before the mixed commission with some interest, supposing that he might give under oath the same statement that he had voluntarily made. It did not surprise me, however, to find that his memory was proved exceedingly treacherous, and has led him into making assertions totally at variance with those stated by myself as coming from him in our interview. In his testimony given in Washington on the 10th of December, 1872, we find the ensuing:

Q. "Have you ever met Gen. Wade Hampton since the war?"

A. "Yes, sir."

Q. "Have you ever discussed with him the subject of the capture and destruction of Columbia?"

A. "I had a conversation with him on that subject."

Q. "Was any one present at the period of this conversation?"

A. "Yes, sir; I think it was Gen. R. K. Scott; someone was there."

Q. "No one else?"

A. "I do not remember."

Q. "You were not aware that there was a newspaper reporter taking down the conversation at the time?"

A. "No, sir, I was not; if I had, I would not have opened my mouth."

Q. "Do you know Mr. DeFontaine?"

A. "No, sir, I never saw him, to my knowledge."

Q. "Do you remember what you said in the course of the conversation?"

A. "No, sir: I don't recall; but I feel perfectly sure that I said almost what I have said in my official report."

Q. "Did you admit or state in the course of that conversation who destroyed Columbia on the night of 17th February, 1865?"

A. "Yes, sir; I think I stated that the Confederate troops set it on fire."

The last answer is italicized to draw special attention to it. Upon reading it I called upon Governor Orr and Gen. Preston for their recollection of this conversation, and received the following answers:

"WASHINGTON, December 21, 1872 – Dear Sir: I have received your letter of the 21st inst, inquiring as to my recollection of what occurred in the executive office in Columbia in 1866 or '67 between yourself and Gen. Howard, of the United States army. I do not remember all that was said, but Gen. Howard said in substance that the city was burned by United States troops; that he saw them fire many houses; and that he tried to arrest the conflagration, and that he regretted the destruction of the city. Without undertaking to give his words, the foregoing contains the substance of what he said relative to the destruction of Columbia. Very respectfully yours,

JAMES L. ORR."

"Gen. Wade Hampton, Baltimore, Md.

"My Dear Sir: I have your note asking me to state my recollection of the conversation between Gen. Wade Hampton and Gen. Howard in presence of Gov. Orr and myself and others. The substance of the conversation was, that Gen. Howard stated and reiterated that no one was authorized to say that the Federal troops did not burn Columbia, for he saw them doing so in numerous instances, in various localities of the town. The conversation was almost exclusively between Gen. Hampton and Gen. Howard, the other persons present saying but very little. Very truly yours, JNO. S. PRESTON"

Mr. Felix DeFontaine, in a late examination before the commission, deposes as follows:

Q. "Please state if you were ever present at an interview between Gens Hampton and Howard, and if yea, when and where, as near as you can state?"

A. "I was present at such an interview. It occurred in the Executive office of James L. Orr, Governor of South Carolina, to the best of my knowledge and belief, in the year 1867."

Q. "At that interview, did you hear Gen. Howard distinctly admit that the firing and destruction of Columbia were the work of the United States troops?"

A. "I did hear Gen. Howard concede that the origin of the fire, and the outrages perpetrated in the city, were the results of the presence of the United States troops. Subsequent to this interview I suggested to Gen. Hampton the propriety of making a record of the fact and its attendant circumstances. I made such a record myself. In explanation of the first part of my present answer, I mean to convey the idea that the destruction was caused by the United States troops."

As confirmation of the statements of these gentlemen, I give the language used by Gen. Howard to the Rev. Mr. Shand, an Episcopal clergyman of Columbia, a man of the highest character and purest piety. The house of this venerable man was burned, and he himself was brutally treated as he was robbed of it. He states that Gen. Howard said to him: "Though Gen. Sherman did not order the burning of the town, yet somehow or other the men had taken up the idea that if they destroyed the capital of South Carolina it would be peculiarly gratifying to Gen. Sherman."

MISSTATEMENTS UNDER OATH

[I]n order to remove every possible doubt, it may well to examine the testimony recently given by Sherman, under oath, before the mixed commission ... On page 65, in his deposition, we find the following:

Q. "Please state where you were when the fire broke out?"

A. "The fire was burning a day and a half or two days before we got into Columbia, but was merely confined to the big bridge across the river, the depot known as the Charleston depot, close by the bridge, and the depot on the opposite side of town, known as the Charlotte depot, and cotton piled up along the various streets, which was burning at least twelve hours before any soldier belonging to my army had gotten within the limits of the city of Columbia."

Now, without discussing the question how he could know so positively as to be able to swear to the fact that cotton was burning at least twelve hours before any of his troops entered the city, we will turn to the proofs to show his misstatements. The bridge across the Congaree is one mile from the Capitol, and at a still greater distance from the business portion of the city. By some misapprehension of orders this bridge was burned during the night of the 15th. This can scarcely be called a fire in the city, as the bridge is outside of the corporate limits, the western terminus being in a different district, Lexington, from the one in which Columbia is situated, which is Richland. Now as to the other points at which Sherman swears that "fires were burning a day and a half or two days" before his entry. The question as to cotton having been then on fire has already been settled by the affidavits heretofore given. As to the other two depots, one was blown up accidentally, as stated by Gen. Beauregard, and was thus fired about 4 o'clock of the morning on which Sherman entered. The testimony already given proves this. The Charlotte depot was fired by orders from headquarters about half past 9 or 10 o'clock A.M. of the same day. These are grave errors to be sworn to before a high tribunal ...

SHERMAN VERSUS SHERMAN

Now ... let us call himself to the stand, as a witness of unblemished character, and unimpeachable veracity, and we shall then have a new case before the public, if not before the Courts— Sherman versus Sherman. In a letter from the defendant [Sherman] in this new case to Benjamin Rawls, of Columbia, which can be found in the published proceedings of Congress somewhere about April, 1866, the following language is used: *"The citizens of Columbia set fire to thousands of bales of cotton rolled out into the streets, and which were burning before we entered Columbia. I myself was in the city as early as 9 o'clock,* and I saw these fires. I saw in your Columbia paper the printed order of Gen. Wade Hampton that on the approach of the Yankee army all the cotton should be thus burned." The italics are mine.

Here is a new version of the story. *"The citizens set fire to thousands of bales."* It seems that I did not set the cotton on fire after all. *"I, myself, was in the city as early as 9 o'clock."* How then does he subsequently swear that he did not enter the city until between 11 or 12?

THE CHARGE AGAINST HAMPTON AN AFTERTHOUGHT

"South Carolina, city of Columbia: Personally appeared before me the Hon. Thomas Jefferson Goodwyn, who, being duly sworn, deposeth and saith that he was mayor of the city of Columbia during the month of February, 1865; that the city was occupied and burned by Gen. Sherman's army on the 17ᵗʰ of February, 1865; than on Sunday, the 19ᵗʰ, he called upon Gen. Sherman, then in Columbia, and was accompanied by the following gentlemen: Rev. N. Talley, Rev. Mr. Connor, Rev. Thomas Rayner, Dr. C. H. Miot, W. M. Martin, Mr. J. J. McCarter and Edwin J. Scott. Gen. Sherman was in good spirits and courteous. A conversation ensued in relation to the burning of the city, in the course of which Gen. Sherman distinctly admitted that his troops had burned the city, but excused them, because, as he alleged, our citizens had given them liquor and made them drunk, whereas they ought to have destroyed the liquor in the city upon the entry of the army. He did not mention or allude to Gen. Hampton or the cotton that had been fired in the streets, nor did he give the slightest intimation, nor make any assertion, that the firing of the city was caused by any order of Gen. Hampton to burn the cotton. Gen. Howard, Gen. Blair, and other Federal officers were present at this interview, which lasted more than half an hour.   T. J. GOODWYN, Late Mayor of Columbia, S.C.

"Sworn to before me, this 24ᵗʰ March, 1868. D. B. Miller, Ex officio Magistrate."

Extracts shall now be given from a letter of the Rev. A. Toomer Porter, an Episcopal clergyman, who was in Columbia when the city was destroyed, dated: "CHARLESTON, August 8, 1866"

"Mr. William J. Rivers, Columbia—My dear Sir: In reply to yours of the 3ʳᵈ, received on the 5ᵗʰ, I will cheerfully comply with the request of the committee appointed by the citizens of Columbia to collect testimony concerning the destruction of Columbia, though the necessity seems passing away inasmuch as Gen. Sherman appears to be discarding the absurd position he took relative to the author of that fearful catastrophe. In a late speech as reported, he seems to admit that he did it, and that it was all right ... While looking at the fire, and thinking how much that was valuable was then being consumed, an officer of the United States army rode up and spoke to me. We had not exchanged many words when Gen. Sherman walked up, still in citizens' clothes. He came from the direction of his headquarters. In the bright light of the burning city he recognized me, and remarked: 'Good evening, Mr. Porter: this is a horrible sight.' 'Yes,' I replied, 'when you reflect that women and children are the victims.' He said, 'Your Governor is responsible for this.' 'How so?' I asked. 'Who ever heard,' he said, 'of an evacuated city to be left a depot of liquor, for an army to occupy? I found one hundred and twenty casks of whiskey in one cellar. Your Governor being a lawyer, or a judge, or something, refused to have it destroyed, as it was private property, and now my men have gotten drunk, they have gotten beyond my control, and this is the result' ... Other cities have been burned, greater losses of property have been met with; to me, the burning of was the least of the horrors. The brutal conduct of that remorseless throng, drunk and sober, officers and men, with but few exceptions; the fearful, sickening agony of suspense and anticipation, the horrible dread of the fate of their helpless women—these things made up the anguish of that awful night; a disgrace to any country and any age, save of barbarism, the blackest page in the dark record of the war. It is due for me to say that I was in Main street when the first bale of cotton took fire, and it occurred from the pipes or cigars of the soldiers who had taken their seats upon it, and the whole of the cotton was burned up early in the day, while the fire commenced at night. Gen. Hampton had told me at daylight, in answer to the question whether he was going to burn the cotton: 'No, if I do so the wind is high, and it might give Sherman an excuse to burn this town.' Yours   very respectfully and truly, A. TOOMER PORTER."

HAZEN'S EVIDENCE AND SHERMAN'S CONFESSION

WASHINGTON, January 28, 1888

Since the above article was written there have appeared several publications which prove fully the main facts stated, and give a few of these as significant. In a "Narrative of Military Service," by Gen. W. B. Hazen, U.S.A., will be found on page 349 the following words used in describing his entry into Columbia: "At about midday my command followed, headed by Gen. Logan and myself. We advanced along Main street, on which Gen. Wood's division was standing at rest with arms stacked, with but few officers present. In this street cotton bales were piled in long lines, and it had been fired by the departing enemy. The engines were on the street and had evidently been at work putting out the fire in the cotton, which still smoked in a few places. The fire was completely under control and was nowhere blazing. A dozen men with tin cups could have managed it." On page 353 he says: "I have never doubted that Columbia was deliberately set on fire in more than a hundred places."

This is the testimony of a Federal officer who was an eye-witness of the scenes he describes, and though he is mistaken, as abundance evidence proves, in stating what was the origin of the fire among the cotton bales, he shows that the fire among the cotton bales, he shows that the fire could not have caused the general conflagration.

The last witness as to whom the responsibility for the destruction of Columbia attaches upon whom I shall call, is Sherman himself, not a credible one in general, but entitled to belief in this case. On p. 288 of his memoirs, these words occur: "Having utterly ruined Columbia, the right wing began its march northward toward Winnsboro on the 20th." When he declares that his army "utterly ruined Columbia," it is scarcely necessary for me to cite further testimony to that fact.

WADE HAMPTON

CHAPTER FIVE

A NIGHT OF HORRORS IN COLUMBIA

AUGUST CONRAD, a native of Germany, immigrated to South Carolina in 1859. He was seventeen when he arrived in Charleston, and sometime after the war began he joined the Charleston Zouave Cadets as a private. In 1862 he found employment with W. C. Bee & Co., a commission merchant firm which engaged in blockade running during the war. Two years later, Conrad took over his brother's position as the Hanoverian Consul. In January 1865, as the army of General Sherman was threatening South Carolina, Conrad traveled to Columbia, thinking that it was a safer place than Charleston, but like so many others, he miscalculated, and soon found himself directly in the path of the enemy.

After the war Conrad returned to Germany, where, in 1879, he published a memoir about the years he spent in South Carolina. His book received little attention at the time, but about twenty years later, three chapters which dealt with the burning of Columbia were translated into English by William H. Pleasants and published as *The Destruction of Columbia, S.C.* The following abridged version of that translation includes Pleasants' preface.

PREFACE

The destruction of the City of Columbia, S.C., in February 1865, by the United States troops under command of General Sherman was an act of barbarity which surpasses all similar acts which are to be found in the long annals of the world's warfare. Columbia, entirely unfortified and undefended, its population consisting entirely of old men, women and children, was surrendered without a blow, under the promise given by the Commanding General of protection to persons and property.

The following description of the destruction of Columbia was written by an eye-witness of that deplorable event—a German gentleman of intelligence and culture. This gentleman had been residing for some years in Charleston, in the capacity of a cotton buyer, and after the outbreak of the Civil War and closing of the ports by blockade, was employed as the secretary and treasurer of the largest company engaged in the business of blockade-running. If the question is asked: "Why, by publishing a detailed description of these horrors, do you revive memories of scenes we would gladly forget?"—the first answer is, that it is due to the truth of history. The Southern writers who have undertaken to write the history of our Civil conflict have not the ear of the world; the Northern writers of history, not only for general reading, but especially of school-books, are notoriously unfair. They write with a strong partisan and political bias—they misrepresent the motives and principles of action of the South, and they err, not simply by the *suppressioveri* [suppressing the truth], but by the *suggestiofalsi* [suggesting falsehoods.]

A second reason why this description of the obliteration of Columbia is published is that very few, except the inhabitants of that ill-fated city, have any just conception of the horrors of that night of incendiarism and robbery; of unchecked license, of insult

74

and every crime mentionable and unmentionable. In the histories above alluded to I doubt whether the destruction of Columbia is mentioned at all; but if noticed, it is lauded as one of the heroic actions of their most admired general. But if heroic and splendid deeds deserve to be painted in glowing words for the admiration and improvement of mankind, surely shameful deeds should not be covered up, but displayed in their naked deformity to the candid judgment of an enlightened world.

Wm. H. Pleasants
Hollins, June, 1902

NARRATIVE OF AUGUST CONRAD:

Danger Threatening

The condition of Charleston became more and more perilous by the bombardment, in which the enemy made progress by the use of guns, larger and of longer range, by renewed attacks with these from the points on the seacoast already won; but particularly by the rapid approach of Sherman's famous army, since it was believed to be their principal object to capture and punish the hated city–the "Cradle of Rebellion"—which had made so stubborn a resistance and prolonged the war by blockade-running.

With the dreaded capture of the seaports, which was now considered only a question of time, the business (blockade-running) must of itself come to an end, and it was now to be considered how to secure to the stockholders in the company their property.

When the catastrophe finally came, all the ships were lucky enough to be found in foreign ports, and after the ensuing peace, which was caused by the subjugation of the South, were then sold for the account of those interested. The ready money on deposit at the banks, and the considerable amount earned by the sale of cotton, which was deposited safe in Liverpool, must, so far as they had not yet been distributed, be paid to the stockholders, and now the duty lay before me, in consideration of that determination, to pay out the dividends by means of checks upon the aforesaid banks, and by drafts on our correspondents in England.

For this purpose I took my position in Columbia. Mr. Bee (the president of the company) wished to hold his in Charleston as long as possible, and to leave Charleston only in the extremest necessity, when his person was in danger, after he had carried his family to a place of safety on one of his plantations in the country, and sent all the movable and indispensable objects of value belonging to his private estate, to his firm, and to the company to Columbia and various other places.

On the 23rd of January, 1865, I left Charleston for the last time, filled, it is true, with anxiety and doubt for the future, but not imagining that I would never see the place again—and that I had probably taken leave forever of the people and the place that had become endeared to me.

In Columbia my two colleagues and I had plenty to do in bringing up the arrears of business resulting from my long absence, and in gratifying our stockholders with their dividends in Confederate money and sterling exchange. My business fully occupied my time, so that it was scarcely possible for me to visit the families that had shown me kindness.

People had actually no fear at all about Columbia; on the contrary, it was supposed that the property which had been sent there was safer than at any other place in the wide Confederacy.

But misfortune travels fast, and as a thunderbolt from the clear sky, at first incredible, but becoming every day more certain, came first the rumor and then the certainty that Sherman had suddenly changed his course, and that the army was marching in the direction of Columbia.

A feeling of horror seized upon the population on account of this news, which had been, until the attainment of certainty, always doubted. If this news was really well-founded, the arrival of dreaded Northern troops could be delayed only a few days. Many private individuals, but particularly the banks and public officials, took flight with the property which had been placed under their protection, which was removed, so far as the railroads could accomplish it, farther into the interior. Madame Rutjes [his landlady] had also run away, and I had to seek another lodging. I rented a room and took my meals at one of the restaurants still left. However, by far the largest portion of the inhabitants could not and would not go away—people did not know where, if not here, they could be safe—where they could find a place of refuge. Besides, it was very questionable whether any great annoyances would be caused to individuals by the impending capture of the place, if indeed that should take place.

I also wrapped myself in a feeling of security too great, and one which, as events proved, was misplaced. I thought to myself that the enemy was not my enemy, and that they would respect my office, as well as the property found under the flag of Hanover. That would certainly have happened if the commanding officers had been able to hold the rabble of troops in subordination and discipline. But I was now convinced that they would bring no trouble upon me, and decided to remain calmly here to await the course of events. My colleagues left me, and betook themselves farther into the interior to the places of refuge of their families. They took a great part of the books and papers with them, because their presence would probably reveal my participation in a forbidden business and bring me annoyance.

The enemy advanced in force, and his immediate arrival in Columbia removed all doubt. On the part of the Confederates, there had been hastily assembled several thousand militia-men for the protection of the city, and with the bales of cotton, at hand and admirably adapted to the purpose, they erected barricades. However useless and injurious the proceeding might be, it was determined to defend a city, open and approachable from every side.

On the fifteenth of February, 1865, the stroke of fate descended. The launching of the thunderbolt caused no greater horror than the terrifying sultriness of the atmosphere which preceded it, while fortunately we did not know what results would follow. Not even now was there any foreboding of the utter destruction that was to follow, and in addition to the anxiety of all, the sight, new and entirely strange to everybody, awakened a certain interest. For myself, particularly, who had no fear for myself and the peaceful population, the warlike scene had a singular charm. I expected an easy, quick capture of the place, the establishment of a garrison of United States troops, and a departure of the army, and accordingly a peaceful, well ordered carrying out of these movements.

On the day above named the enemy appeared on the heights on the other side of the river, and the busy activity of an army of about sixty thousand men with their artillery, wagon-train, tents, etc., clearly visible with the naked eye from the city, presented a highly interesting sight. It seemed as if the troops had chosen this delightful spot, and wished to rest from their exhausting marches. The trees, which partly covered this plateau in every direction, were cut down, the ground leveled, tents were set up, and a bivouac established, in which there seemed to be as much activity as in an anthill—out of which the flames and smoke of the camp-fires ascended—and out of which the drum and trumpet signals resounded. It seemed to be a holiday and rest day for the troops, or, perhaps, a strengthening and preparation for hard work; for they could not know what defensive works were opposed to them, after the surrender of the city, which had been demanded through a flag-of-truce, was declined.

It was said that General Sherman, when he arrived at this point, in his humorous style, addressed his soldiers in about the following words: "Boys, down there lies a pretty town; we have, for a long time, had no good lodging; there can we find it; and it would be really a good thing, if we took a close look at this place, and if it pleases us, take possession of it. What say you to that?"

The "boys" must have agreed to this, and expressed their approbation by a unanimous "Hip! hip! hurrah!"

The day passed entirely undisturbed; the enemy was able to grant that boon in his certainty of victory. On our side the barricades were vigorously pushed forward, and time gained for removing a great deal of property.

A NIGHT OF TERROR

Night fell upon the once peaceful city, in which to-day wild disorder and uproar reigned; upon the wicked enemy, who with so many thousand agents was employed in its utter extinction, upon the unfortunate human creatures, who in distress and anxiety were looking forward to the future. To whom could such a night as this yield rest and refreshment?

As darkness set in, the soldiers bivouacing in the streets kindled fires to cook their suppers. I made to the captain at our house a plea in this regard, whether this lighting of fires should not be forbidden, since cotton lying around in the immediate vicinity and various other inflammable materials scattered around might easily be set on fire, and a great disaster ensue. *O sancta simplicitas!* How could I expect any consideration from these men? The answer of the captain, "What had I to do with the handling of the troops?—would I place a kitchen at their disposal for the preparation of their food?" threw me back into proper submissiveness. I dared not stir up to personal enmity the man who alone possessed one spark of dignity and authority. I invited him and his two lieutenants to partake of our frugal supper; but before it was ready a new event arrested our attention: a mighty column of fire and smoke was rising at some distance from us: a railroad depot on the other side of the city was on fire, and the cotton stored there gave abundant nutriment to the flames. This calamity, too! And just on this day! But in the excitement this occurrence made little impression, till in the opposite direction too, fire broke out, and when a few minutes later a house took fire and that, too, immediately behind the one inhabited by us, then the conviction dawned upon us, that it was a prearranged firing of the city of incalculable consequences, and this thought filled us with horror.

The fact that the enemy lounging around the burning houses made not the smallest effort to extinguish the fire, but amused themselves with insulting remarks at the sight, confirmed us in the belief that the city was intentionally fired, and from that time until the present day I do not know whether the firing done by the rabble was ordered by the higher powers or only permitted.

Under such circumstances the further spread of the fire was inevitable, and we were obliged to leave our dwelling. The poor widow to whom no possibility offered itself of saving her possessions was in despair. On her knees she besought the commander of the men quartered in the house to conduct herself and her little children to a place of safety, and through his men cause to be transported to a family of her acquaintance, with whom she wished to take refuge, at least a part of her property. In a certain way this man complied with this entreaty, which might have softened a stone. He escorted the unfortunate lady and her children with a few articles of value, principally silverware, which they themselves could carry, but any further assistance he could not and would not render. What we could hastily gather up and pack in bundles, trunks, and boxes, we then carried downstairs, in order to remove it either by ourselves, if possible, or relying upon the assistance of the captain and his men. But as soon as a piece was brought down, the hungry pack seized upon it and carried it off, or divided its contents before our eyes, and every further attempt ended with the same result.

The captain declared that he could do nothing with this state of things, and so we were compelled to resign ourselves to the inevitable. All that we asked was, that he would extend his personal protection to the lady now almost frightened to death. I loaded myself with my tin box and different bundles and packets, made up from the contents of my traveling bag and from the articles previously brought here, and left the house already on fire, with the poor family, whom I had now to leave to their fate, and must think about my own security, if that were in any way possible.

Loaded in this way, holding in my hands, under my arms, my own property and that entrusted to me, I was determined to seek shelter in the house of the family of McCully, friends of mine, though a long distance off, yet the nearest place at which I could find refuge. I avoided the direct course over the principal streets, in which a great throng of noisy, exulting soldiers was moving, who were amusing themselves with setting bales of cotton on fire, I hoped to reach my destination without danger on the streets that were more quiet. The city presented an inexpressibly horrible aspect. A large majority of the houses in every direction were now burning, and the wind contributed to the rapid spread of the destroying, element. In the houses, on the streets, the infamous rabble plundered, destroyed, and raged as the Wild Hunt, just as if hell had broken loose. In the midst of all this was heard the heart-rending cry of distress of human beings, stripped by the robbers, at times, of those personally assaulted or endangered by the fire. Here and there these hapless creatures, with little children in their arms or with their small possessions, were seen running from the devils and the fire, seeking protection anywhere, but only to run in their supposed place of refuge upon new destruction. It was horrible! And the conviction of the poor, perplexed creatures that they could not save themselves made the situation only more frightful.

But nobody could give them help—everybody must be thinking of his own fate, of securing his own safety if possible; and so I could not trouble myself about what was going on around me, but must seek to escape from this scene of horror—to follow up the slight beam of hope of perhaps accidental betterment. In my course which I took by a wide circuit through back streets, I was at first fortunate enough to lose only the smaller packets carried under my arm, and which I could not hold on to fast enough, inasmuch as they were snatched by some soldiers that I met. My hands grasped tightly their burden, and several attempts to take it from me were unsuccessful, and by rapid flight I escaped the different robbers who, strange to say, desisted from an energetic pursuit, and waited for a more convenient opportunity of robbery. Such opportunities presented themselves in rich abundance.

I had almost reached my destination, and found the neighborhood in which my place of refuge lay as yet entirely spared by the fire. A gleam of hope of relief from anxiety and distress grew to a joyful anticipation, that I would at last find rest, and in my excited brain arose all the possible plans as to where and how I should conceal my property, perhaps bury it, in order to escape the search of the sleuth-hounds.

Then a company of soldiers in regular march under the command of a captain, and which as I supposed was performing patrol duty, suddenly crossed my path, and I was childishly simple enough to look upon them, not as a band of thieves, but as protectors of the persecuted. Therefore, I slackened my running, which had already exhausted me, and met this detachment at a street corner, hoping to finish the rest of my journey under their protection, as they turned into my street.

But I was halted and asked by the Captain what I was carrying there with me. I told that I was the Hanoverian Consul, and declared that my baggage consisted partly of my private property, and partly of papers belonging to the Consulate, saved with great difficulty from the fire. By that I believed I had sufficiently established my character, and might venture to proceed on my way. But the Captain was inquisitive, and wished to convince himself of the truth of my statement. Then my baggage was taken away from me, I was made to open the box—the whole company rummaged the satchels—threw the contents out, one took this, another that—and left only the empty box and satchels, the Consulate seal and several letters and worthless papers. All protests, all entreaties were in vain, and my exclamation of despair on account of the great loss, which at the moment of excitement I could not repress, was silenced by the threat to shoot me dead, if I did not keep quiet.

Not content with the result of this robbery, the Captain demanded also my *portemonnaie* and watch, and submissive, as I was, in view of the violence threatening me, and in order thereby to escape a thorough search of my person, I gave him what he demanded.

That, kind reader, was the function of a patrol of the famous army of Sherman, which army was attended with the general sympathy of the Germans (not of the English and French) in their war of devastation against the noble-minded, fair-dealing Southerners. That was a specimen of the robber bands—the officers, who were led into the field against a spirited, but noble enemy, and displayed their bravery in base, dastardly robbery, insult and injury of defenseless human beings, especially women and children. I refrain from all exaggeration in my description and I leave it to everybody to form his own opinion; at the same time I am willing to declare, that not all, perhaps only the smaller part of the Northern troops was made up of such offscourings of humanity, because I later had the opportunity to become acquainted with brave, well-disciplined soldiers of the United States.

I gathered up the box and the few remaining papers, and then gradually the full knowledge of my loss dawned upon me. The loss of the valuables entrusted to me by my brother, from whom nearly all that he had earned by long years of hard work was taken, and who in a foreign land was resting in full confidence in the safety of his possessions, affected me most. This would certainly be a severe blow to him. Furthermore, this loss consisted of a large part of the exchange on England, which I had made out for the stock-holders of the Company, and which had not been called for by them, representing a very large sum. There was for a long time no possibility of stopping the payment of the drafts, and making them worthless for their unlawful possessors; in the meantime these drafts might already have been paid in good faith to the thief and his accomplices.

The loss of the papers belonging to the Consulate and the Company troubled me less; that of my own, in comparison with these above-mentioned, not at all. But I was prostrated by the far-reaching loss, and by the impossibility of doing anything for the recovery of anything. I experienced this night, and once later, how much a man can endure, but also how much less frightful is the presence—the certainty of so hard a stroke of fate, than the apprehension of it, if one has reached the conclusion that he is not able to remedy it, and that he must be resigned.

When I became clearly convinced of the fact, my despair changed to quiet resignation. A slight consolation lay in the thought that in this hour so many people were visited with far harder misfortune than I. In all that I had passed through, I could yet consider myself at least fortunate, in having saved my life, the valuables secreted about my person, and the papers still left in the satchels, for whose further security I, of course, had reason to fear.

With the little that was left me, I arrived safe at the house of the McCullys, but in an exhausted and depressed state. The poor family were, in view of the important events, of the danger in which they were involved, but which they had had so far escaped, in great alarm, and they greeted my appearance with joy. The husband, disabled in body and mind, sat buried in silent brooding; an aged grandmother lay sick in bed, and the recent frightful occurrences were very carefully concealed from her; and with great difficulty I made them take measures for the collecting and temporarily securing their most valuable objects, in order that in the event of a sudden attack, or of the fire getting there, they might be ready for flight, and for taking with them the most valuable of their possessions.

These good people had the good luck to find among the soldiers who had quartered themselves in the house a brave, educated young man who was not only entirely respectful and amiable towards the inmates, but defended them, as well as their property against the vile thieves who forced themselves in. As a matter of course the man stood quite alone among his comrades in the strength of his character and virtue; he defied them as well as his superior officers, in their repeated attempts to rob and set fire to the house, until his strength no longer held out against the rude violence. He denounced the conduct of his comrades as vile, shameful; he deplored that so many good-for-nothing scoundrels, consisting mostly of Europeans (Irish and Dutch), were among them; he protested, however, that the horrible deeds were committed against the orders of the highest authorities.

The flames were now raging in this part of the city, at first more protected, after the houses which promised to yield booty were robbed and destroyed. The rush of the valiant men became stronger and stronger, and in a short time our brave defender was unable to drive back the highway robbers storming the doors and windows. All obstacles were broken down; what was useful was carried off; what was useless to them destroyed, and with a few possessions only was I able, in company with the poor unfortunate creatures, to get out of the house. Already the flames were pouring out of the windows. It was a matter of great difficulty to save the old grandmother, who escaped death by fire by a hair's breadth, and was carried out by two negroes who were kind enough to lend a helping hand. I caught one of the noble heroes by the throat at the moment when he was about to set fire to the bed on which the old lady lay, because I had run thither at her shriek of horror and stopped, just at the right time, this fearful murder. In the struggle, which in view of this incredible crime I did not fear, in the exchange of words which was inevitable, I found out, to my horror, that the beast was a German who could not even speak English. Such a son then has our good Fatherland sent for the extirpation of slavery, but in reality for robbery and murder. And alas, he was not the only one of his race among them who practiced such shameful deeds.

It was the favorite plan of the scoundrels, when they had thoroughly plundered the house, to set fire to the beds. By that means their object was best accomplished; the fire spread quickly, and the rogues had no reason to fear that a single thing would be spared.

And so again burnt out, again without shelter, I left with the family of the McCullys, whose house was no on fire, too, in several places, lighting for its inhabitants of many years their sorrowful, homeless way. But whither should we betake ourselves? There was no longer any great room for choice; only comparatively few houses were left uninjured, and these, too, in all probability, would be visited with the same horrible fate. I determined yet once more to seek safety, and go to my friends, the Gronings, for shelter. The Arsenal Hill was as yet wrapped in deep darkness, and thither the band of incendiaries had not yet forced their way, or had found the houses there, which were mostly small and unpretentious, unworthy of their attention. And so my friends had still a home. A part of my fugitive companions—the old grandmother—the invalid father (both of whom a short time after this horrible night died from the effects of it, perhaps, too, of hunger), and besides two daughters found shelter with relations, in the close vicinity to my destination—the mother with two other daughters accompanied me to the Groning's house, which we fortunately reached, but not without having lost on the way the greatest part of the property taken with us.

I was finally stunned in the presence of repeated calamities, in the presence of the strokes of fate, which in the last hours, which seemed to me an eternity, had broken in upon me, and in the presence of the splendidly horrible sight of the sea of fire, which seen from the hill, spread out under me, out of which a wild confusion of voices arose. I thought now only of myself and the unfortunates committed to my protection to whom, alas, I had been able to afford so little help.

And so one part of the family was temporarily sheltered, and I, with the others, was received at the house of our friends. They, in some unaccountable way, with the exception of anxiety and terror, had received no injury—had been able to ward off the numerous visits of the intruders. In particular, the energetic Mrs. Groning, a most amiable lady, knew how to repulse the cowardly rabble by her fearless deportment, by her severe reproof, and by word pictures of their damnable doings; she, herself a Northern woman, in the presence of the sleuth-hounds, renounced all connection with a people who employed such a rabble in their service, and her rapid, energetic way of talking produced a powerful effect upon those men, who had not expected such a reception, where in other cases they had met with only terror, trembling, and entreaty. These negotiations, carried on through closed doors and windows, always ended with the departure of the robbers, who sought an easier field for their industry.

It was in the early hours of the morning, when I reached my new asylum completely exhausted, and with my unfortunate companions was bidden welcome. My overstrained nerves refused any farther service, and I could no longer stand upright. Stretched out on the carpet of my chamber, I found a little rest that I needed so much, and forgot, for a while, the trials I had passed through, and those now surrounding me, but continually being roused by new disturbers of my peace, and expecting to be driven away again.

The uninvited visits were all the time slackening, and at daybreak they ceased altogether. The contemptible creatures seemed at last to be content with the result of their devilish work— or they were tired out with the exertions of the night—or they themselves shuddered at the sight of the devastation they had made, which the daylight brought to their view, or perhaps they were called to other service. Suffice it to say, we were no longer disturbed, the streets were cleared, and we breathed again! It seemed really as if the kindly cottage had enjoyed singular good fortune to be preserved from the general destruction, and after all that had happened we were thankful for this favor of heaven, which had left to our good hosts their home and their property, and afforded to us a comfortable shelter at least, while so many unfortunates were obliged to do without this shelter, and that too in the most inclement season of the year.

After I had recovered from the first shock, I realized my whole loss, and notwithstanding the considerable amount of it, recognized how well I had fared in comparison with many others— e .g., the McCully family robbed of everything (I had saved my money, jewels, etc.). I went out to look after the other portion of that family and Mrs. Volger, who had been separated from me in the early part of the night, and find out what fate had befallen them. I found her fortunately concealed in one of the places of refuge she had sought, and though she was hardly alive from terror, from the loss she had suffered, still a great blessing was vouchsafed to her, too, by an accident.

These facts were, under the circumstances, almost tranquilizing to myself and to the relations, and when I had brought them this news, I made an examination of the devastation of the last night.

CAPTURE OF COLUMBIA

In the early morning of the following day the scene changed. In consequence of the refusal to surrender, the enemy began to bombard the city, without causing any considerable damage, it is true, but yet putting the population into new alarm. I just escaped death, or a severe injury, from a fragment of a bombshell about the size of a walnut, which exploded immediately before my feet, and buried itself several inches in the ground, and which, in spite of my terror, I dug up, and still have as a trophy of remembrance of that memorable day, and the danger which I happily escaped.

The prearranged resistance, the defense of the city by the small force, was an absurd, nay frightful resolution on the part of the Commander of the Confederate forces, and, under the existing circumstances, met with no approval from the people of Columbia. Whether he had seen the entire futility of such defense, or had assented to the desire of the worthy old Mayor, the handful of Confederates withdrew, the railroads carried away their last wagons and implements and the Mayor himself went into the enemy's camp, and announced the unconditional surrender of the city, requesting at the same time for it and its inhabitants respectful treatment and protection.

I had in the meanwhile arranged my affairs as well as was possible; had secured the property belonging to the company, which was left behind in a fire-proof safe in the office, had packed my private property in a trunk, and committed it to the care of my landlord. The most important papers and objects of value belonging to myself, my brother, the company and the Consulate, I had placed, partly in a large tin box, and partly in my different satchels, and also filled a traveling bag with clothing and other indispensable articles, in order to keep it by me under all circumstances. I carried in a broad leather belt around my body under my clothing, the sum of about six hundred dollars in gold, which I had reserved for possible needs, besides the jewels that I had bought, representing a considerable value, and different interest coupons.

Provided with these treasures and with the royal flag of Hanover, I betook myself to the residence of a German lady, whom I had known in Charleston, who had established herself her in her profession of teacher of music and singing, and who, in anticipation of coming events, in her anxiety about herself and several little children, had begged me, by virtue of my office or in person, to protect her.

Accordingly I brought my baggage temporarily here, displayed the banner of Hanover from the window, and after I believed the office and the residence well protected, I awaited the course of events.

Towards midday then the entrance of the enemy's troops began. First, there was a detachment of pioneers, which removed the obstructions that blocked the broad principal street, after the object of the barricades, a bloody street fight was happily avoided. All the obstructions in sight were thrown aside, and the carriage of the Mayor with him and several higher officers drove through the now unobstructed streets to the City Hall. The great army followed in seemingly endless columns, and at its head General Sherman, energetic and calmly gazing around, with his staff and all the blue coated regiments from the Northwestern States of the Union—

infantry, cavalry, and artillery. The entire army marched into the city and distributed themselves in the different streets; however, some of them marched through, and because the city did not furnish room enough for all, established themselves in the environs.

I must declare I was delighted at the spectacle—the endless, heaving multitude, which had before and behind them so long and so difficult marches—the famous and dreaded leader with his brilliant staff— the streaming banners of the mighty, victorious Union. All this was to me new and highly interesting, and I do not regret to have experienced it, even though I would like to refuse to recall scenes of like nature.

The troops were in the highest spirits, sang and were noisy by ranks and companies, cast longing and scornful looks at the houses, and, doubtless, thought of the treasures therein hidden, which might fall to them as good booty.

The inhabitants of Columbia were submissive in their calamity and hardly looked out of the windows at the entrance of the enemy. The capture of this city so peaceable—of this point so important for the Confederates, filled me with sorrow; the thought of what might result therefrom to it filled me with anxiety; but everybody must patiently submit to the inevitable. The streets were entirely deserted by civilians and the new masters bore themselves insolently in their brute force.

I will for the honor of General Sherman, and the whole United States, assume, that the troops were, in accordance with what is customary in all civilized nations and armies, ordered not to seize private property, nor destroy it—not to molest peaceful citizens, especially ladies, and that the commanding officers really intended to extend to the city officials the promised defense—even protection of every person and of every private possession, and that, accordingly, the events which turned out to the contrary were to be ascribed only to the rough rabble as committed against all orders and against all decency. But, after all, the responsibility for the outrages committed by their underlings belongs to the leaders, and must sully their fame, either because Sherman's army was destitute of subordination and discipline, or, if these existed, that the officers permitted these shameful deeds, perhaps in secret took pleasure therein.

After the formal entry into the city had come to an end, and the higher officers, i. e., only the generals and the colonels were quartered in some of the better class of houses which had been abandoned by their inhabitants, or which had been voluntarily vacated by them for this purpose, the rest of the crowd of soldiers seemed to be left entirely to themselves. The soldiers bivouaced in the streets, or took possession of the houses left unoccupied, where they established themselves comfortably; but the inhabited houses too were not spared, and, next in order, they took lodging on the floors of the houses, in the front yards and galleries. So far this was all very well, and was rather respectful treatment, inasmuch as inhabited rooms were not invaded.

In the house, too, in which I had taken up my abode, soldiers swarmed, among them several officers, and these were somewhat polite, and respected the flag; and the Captain in command gave the assurance that nothing should be taken from us and that we must remain quietly in our rooms. But the billeting of men in the house was by no means agreeable; the jeering and coarse language of the soldiers, their entire behavior, their insolent demands for food and drink to which they were not entitled, but in which they were satisfied as far as was possible, troubled us very much. Everywhere there were unruly, shabby fellows that could not fail to produce disgust and terror in everybody, collected from lowest orders of humanity, from every nation in the world, among whom, with the exception of the Americans from the interior, the Irish and Germans were most numerous. To the shame of the German nation must I, with sorrow declare, that its sons that belonged to this army were the foremost and most active in the shameful deeds which were afterwards done; and of this fact I had, on many occasions, the opportunity to convince myself.

We could from our windows, that opened on the principal street, see the low, savage, and disgusting conduct of the troops, and I became immediately convinced that there was no good to be expected from them, (and) that the Confederate soldiers, nearly all sons of the Southland, were far superior, in manners, discipline, and courage, to this assemblage of hirelings. I speak with entire impartiality, and I admit exceptions the more willingly, since such exceptions afterwards became known to me from the statements of others and my own experience; but in the main it was a band of thieves and robbers, the inferior officers included.

The gangs of thieves soon, no longer contented with the occupation of streets and houses, and with the gifts voluntarily offered, or obtained by begging, began, as a preliminary, to break open and plunder the stores and warehouses which were all closed. Only the money which perhaps they found, and the articles of value in gold and silver were taken; everything else was rummaged, torn to pieces, ruined and scattered around. It presented a sad appearance, when all conceivable objects, which the soldiers could not use, or carry off with them, disappeared from the different stores, lay scattered in the streets, and were here trodden under foot and destroyed. What could and should unlucky owners do against this rude violence? Scorn and vile words were the least that the owners, when they arrived at the scene of their ruin, gained by protest, by entreaty, especially as an appeal to officers there present and co-operating had not the slightest effect.

Seeing this open plundering, I naturally feared a similar fate for the property belonging to myself and the company at the places where I had left them. Anxiety and curiosity drove me out among the mad throng to inform myself in regard to their fate. The somewhat out-of-the-way office I found undisturbed, and besides, the breaking open of a good safe was not to be considered an easy matter, which (safe) moreover contained nothing of special value, after the books and papers were removed, and my own valuable papers were placed under my own protection. Satisfied on this point, I betook myself to my logdings, and afterwards emptied a closely packed traveling bag, in order to fill it, if it were yet possible, with a portion of the contents of my trunk, because it seemed to me that the things were safer in my immediate vicinity than in the unprotected room. I had moved only a few steps with the empty bag, when I was halted by a mounted soldier, or robber, with the order to hand it over to him. My remonstrance that it did not belong to him, but to me, that I would like myself to keep possession of my property, was not noticed by the hero, but he drew and brandished his sabre, with the remark that I must not take up his valuable time, but rather save my arm. I saw the justice of this good advice, and followed it by giving up the bag , now, fortunately, empty. That was the first highway robbery that I experienced. Worse things were to happen to me.

In my lodgings a new horror awaited me. On entering the yard I found the contents of my trunk, so far, at least, they still existed, were scattered around and mixed up with strange objects: little negro children were amusing themselves with the broken pictures of my relations, and playing with the objects which the thieves had thrown aside as useless to them. Letters of my friends, which I had preserved so carefully, which contained such cheering words of love and consolation, were here in publicity thrown about soiled and torn. Many valuable and irreplaceable objects were entirely lost, and a feeling of sadness at this sudden loss of my property, mixed with rage and contempt towards the vile destroyers, took possession of me. I gathered the most valuable remnants, so much as I could take care of, and gave up all that was left to utter destruction. My landlady had fared as badly as I; her personal intervention had not availed to protect her own property and mine, and the loss of her silverware, which she previously had prudently buried in her garden, and which she believed to be safe, affected her far more seriously than myself.

I now hurried back to my temporary quarters and found here in the house of Mrs. Volger as yet no trouble, while the store situated on the ground floor was already completely gutted. I do not know whether we had to attribute the protection up to this time, to the flag, or to good luck, or to the somewhat respectable garrison, of the house; however that may be, we conceived the hope that we would not be exposed to any further danger.

Madder and madder became the tumult in the streets—partly from exultation over the booty they had gotten, partly curses and abusive language on the part of those who had been deceived in their expectations. The commanding officers remained entirely passive amid these open robberies, although to some families, who had courage enough to make complaint at headquarters of the indignities which were becoming more and more outrageous, a guard was given for the protection of their houses. But only *pro forma*, and in every case without effect, because either sufficient authority was not given to these guards, or because they did not obey; the most of the houses so guarded suffered the common fate.

I had not been able to interest myself in behalf of the families with whom I was on friendly terms, on account of the remoteness of their residences: everybody had enough to do for himself, and I did not venture to go so far from my lodgings.

Thus the day ended for the noble warriors in pleasant, profitable work; but there was no holiday evening for them—the time was too valuable for that—the night was far better suited to black souls—it only afforded further assistance to their dark doings.

RESULTS OF THE DEVASTATION

The beautiful, peaceful city of Columbia was no more! In one single night, yea, in a few hours, it had disappeared, and been converted into ruins! Only a few houses on Arsenal Hill and in the farthest outskirts of the city remained standing; the whole of the interior portion was entirely destroyed. The spaces where yesterday streets intersected the city were no longer passable, and only in some places to be recognized by the walls still standing. Everything else was a great heap of ruins, out of which rose a smoke, poisoning the air. With renewed horror, with disgust and hate for the perpetrators and the permitters of these outrages, I gazed at ruins of the place which had become so dear to me, which now in its new and horrifying aspect was no longer recognizable. My office, too, with its contents, my dwelling place, and so many homes, at which I had spent many pleasant hours, lay buried under the ruins!

And the men who yesterday were without foreboding, and the inmates of these former houses! A great many of them had been lost in the tempest of fire, and were now laying accusation against their murderers before the throne of the Most High. The bodies of those who had perished in the flames were some time afterwards found, removed from the mountains of rubbish and buried.

And the survivors? Whither had terror and distress driven them? Those who had not been so fortunate, as I had been, to find shelter among friends (and comparatively few could be taken in by those whose houses were spared), had been driven by despair into the woods; and now imagine such a situation—how many thousands of human beings, of all ages and conditions, white and black, wandering the forest in the dark night, seeing no possibility of protecting themselves against the cold wind, of feeding and clothing themselves, since they have saved nothing but their bare lives! How families were separated, mothers and children calling for each other, neither knowing whether their loved ones were in safety, or had fallen a sacrifice to the dreadful fire!

Yes, dear reader, that is an awful picture—it sounds incredible, seems an exaggeration; but so it was in reality, in our age of the world, in a civilized land; and caused by those, who out of pure philanthropy (?) wished to procure for the slaves glorious freedom, and to that end employed such means as placed their wards themselves, along with their masters, who were hated by the so-called liberators, but loved by the slaves, in boundless misery.

The fall of Columbia stands quite unique in the history of the American war, but it was sufficient to sully the principle, the conduct, and the results of it, and must for many generations entail the hate of the South Carolinians towards their Northern brethren, who brought upon their forefathers such atrocious treatment.

I give my opinion with entire impartiality, in accordance with my own experiences, and from personal observation of the frightful scenes and I doubt not, that anyone who will calmly consider the matter, will agree with me in my judgment of the shameful conduct of the army of the United States, even though the foregoing description may have imperfectly pictured the horrifying experiences and boundless wretchedness resulting therefrom.

And the slaves ... [T]he victors troubled themselves not a single moment about them; they had endured the same fate as the whites, suffered like losses and privations. They remained faithful to their masters, who shared with them their last piece of bread, without being under the least obligation to do so. How much assistance will, I am sure, at this time (1879) be granted to the negroes by their former masters, without which they must perish, and which was not extended to them at that time by their liberators, by the champions of a principle which was at least commendable. Accordingly these champions deliberately abandoned their proteges to the misery, to which they had condemned them, left them to pine, as before, in the slavery from which they had come to save them. Their oppressors, on the contrary, from feelings of humanity, cared for them, that in their condition of freedom they might not starve to death.

And the noble warriors for freedom and the rights of man—the robbers, thieves, and incendiaries? They had to-day left the scene of their shameful conduct, and spread themselves for the most part over the surrounding country, there to seek booty in cattle and provisions, to lay waste the land, and above all to destroy the railroads for a distance of many miles. Only a comparatively few were left behind as a garrison for the place and guard of headquarters. The robbing and burning of the few remaining houses had ceased, as I suppose, by the strict orders of the commanding officers, in whom, in view of the existing devastation, a little compassion might have been awakened, and who now were in a position to maintain discipline.

There was, however, all the time a considerable number of disgusting figures, who still lingered in the place once called

Columbia, who were busily engaged in rummaging the piles of debris, and seeking for the melted gold and silver; likewise in digging up the ground in the gardens and yards of the few remaining houses, to find the treasures which were possibly there hidden. They were in this work amply rewarded, and the booty, which was afterwards carried away by them, consisting principally of gold and silver, and objects of value requiring little room, must have been enormous, as an entire train of transport wagons was filled with them.

I have thus attempted to describe how these men became possessed of the stolen property, how the city was destroyed contrary to the custom of all civilized nations, how the peaceful inhabitants were robbed of their property, reduced to poverty and suffering, nay, even murdered, just as I was forced to live through these deeds and observe the consequences. But even more horrifying accounts of individual cases, which I did not see, afterwards came into publicity. It was not alone that the band of robbers demanded the surrender of money, watches, and valuables; no—they did not take time for that; in many instances they possessed themselves of such articles by force; the breastpins were snatched from the breasts of ladies, the rings from their fingers, and the earrings from their ears; they did not restrain themselves till the opening of the jewel cases, but lacerated the ears and tore off the clothing from the bodies of the trembling women. I have myself seen a lady with the lobes of both ears torn asunder. What outrages in word and deed the female sex in many cases had to suffer, I will here only hint.

I draw a veil over the horrible past, which would seem to me a bad dream, if it had not wrought its lasting effect upon my future; and if I am in the fortunate condition to be obliged only once, and for a short time, to lift the veil, in order to impress those moments on my remembrance in my description, the greatest part of my fellow sufferers were not, and perhaps not even now are, in the condition to cover up with other thoughts that night of horror, or to escape its consequences.

After the first excitement had somewhat subsided, and there was calmness enough to reflect upon the state of affairs, anxiety for the future began to press upon me and to put me in embarrassment in regard to taking the necessary steps. It seemed, in the first place, incumbent upon me to give my chief information of the disaster, and get from him new instructions; then also to inform our correspondent in Liverpool of the robbery of the drafts drawn upon him, and stop the payment of them; furthermore, I wished to gain certain knowledge of the place of retreat of our bookkeeper with the books of the company, and finally to leave a place in which I was now only a burden.

I had no idea how an escape from the place, or intercourse with the outside world might be effected, or whether the Unionists would establish a post here; and on that point I desired first to inform myself of their intentions. I went to the headquarters, which were established in one of the remaining houses, partly to get information about the future of the ruined city, partly to lay complaint about the treatment to which I had been subjected, and perhaps be indemnified for my losses. I did not dare, of course, to let the Union officer know of my participation in the business of blockade-running, because I would have been regarded and treated as an open enemy of the United States; I could appear only as the Consul of Hanover, if I wished to accomplish anything.

I was politely received by General Howard, the next in command under Sherman, who had formerly been a clergyman, had in the Mexican war lost an arm, and who subsequently farther distinguished himself in the Indian war; and my complaint as to the treatment which I had received, as the Consul of a neutral nation, as to the losses, and the robbery of the papers belonging to the Consulate and all of my private property was patiently listened to. The General expressed his regret at the occurrences of the night before and at my passive participation therein, and declared to me, that if I would point out the regiment to which the Captain who had robbed me belonged, he would find him out and have him shot before my eyes. Unfortunately I could not comply with his request, and perhaps the scoundrel enjoys even at this moment his miserable existence. What indeed was the guilt of one single individual in comparison with the innumerable and far greater crimes of many thousands?

I do not know whether the expressed sympathy of the General was only pretended, or really sincere; it made, however, an agreeable impression upon me, and though I could secure no indemnification for, or replacement of my losses—a result which from the very beginning I had not ventured to hope for—yet one proposition of the General seemed to me acceptable. He informed me frankly that the army would leave its present position in a few days, and that no garrison would be left behind; that it would march forward in a northeasterly direction, and would probably, in from eight to fourteen days arrive at a seaport; that, if I wished to avail myself of the opportunity of reaching that point in safety, in order from there to embark for the North or Europe, I might partake of all the comforts and privations of himself and his staff, which I was invited to join; in return for which I would, perhaps, be expected to do some clerical work.

This invitation was by no means to be rejected, and while I cherished an inextinguishable hate towards the band of robbers, yet I would not be disturbed by, had nothing to fear from them, on account of my belonging to the staff, which was, doubtless, composed of respectable men. I, therefore, accepted the proposal provisionally, and had me a pass made out to that effect.

Upon closer consideration, however, I renounced this alluring opportunity. If by this means I should reach Northern territory, I would be able, undoubtedly, to send to England by the quickest, most convenient, and safest way, the information which seemed to me very necessary to be sent or even to reach my home, for I had also formed this plan, because the business was broken up and no longer needed me. But on the other hand, by this course the Confederate territory would be closed to me, and if Charleston still belonged to it, it would be impossible for me to get to that city or to my chief, who I supposed was there, to give him information of my misfortunes. I felt it to be needful for me before everything else, to speak with him, to lay before him a full account of my last experiences and of the loss sustained. I would not have liked, for any consideration, to have been brought before him in suspicion that I had only pretended a robbery—that I, perhaps, had embezzled something, or, generally speaking, that I had neglected my duty in any respect. This explanation would not be at all difficult in a personal description of the events; afterwards, I could, with his consent, with a clear conscience pursue my design of seeking my dear home, to which I was now drawn with redoubled longing. Therefore, I determined to remain here and wait for a suitable opportunity by which the accomplishment of my desire might be effected.

On the 20th of February Sherman's army left Columbia, if one will apply that term to the heap of ruins, after having the day before, by order of the commanding general, blown up the arsenal which had been up to this time spared. In that act there was no cruelty, inasmuch as that building was public property, for the destruction of which the right belonged to the victorious enemy. The soldiers continued to be well behaved, and made no further attacks upon persons and upon the property that was still left, but confined themselves to the before-mentioned digging in the ground.

The departure of the troops attracted little attention, and made little impression upon those who were left behind them. After the entire deliverance from them, the people could for the first time clearly think about their real needs, and devise possibly new measures for their removal. I saw the heroes march away, who had in this campaign gathered withered, malodorous laurels—the victorious army which had certainly contributed much to the subjugation of the South, to the finishing of the war, and to the accomplishment of an object noble in principle. But without considering the great bloodshed, the utter misery in which the land was placed, from which it cannot even to-day revive, the means employed were in the highest degree objectionable. "Hail! Columbia, Happy Land," the national hymn of the United States, sounded like mockery from the departing troops to the City of Columbia, totally destroyed by them, and it was a relief to every spirit, however depressed, when the blue forms and their endless train of wagons disappeared in the distance, although they had now nothing more to fear from them.

CHAPTER SIX

SHERMAN'S ARMY IN FAIRFIELD DISTRICT

AFTER LEAVING MUCH of the city of Columbia in ashes, Sherman's forces moved across the Saluda and Broad Rivers into Fairfield District. The town of Winnsboro, which was located here, suffered as many other South Carolina communities did during this fateful time in the state's history. On April 18th, about two months after the invaders left, a Winnsboro newspaper published the following account by a writer identifying himself as "J.B."

INVASION OF FAIRFIELD DISTRICT BY SHERMAN

About the 18th of February, immediately after the fall of Columbia, Sherman's army entered the southwestern boundary of Fairfield, sweeping over it like a hurricane or tornado, carrying destruction in its progress, leaving behind it smoking ruins and an insulted robbed people, many impoverished families and desolated homes. Long will the inhabitants remember the last ten days of February, 1865. A People are not likely to forget the memorable period when they were pillaged and plundered and perhaps burned out. They can never forget the day when their homes—upon which they had spent the labor of a lifetime, and where they had collected many comforts and cherished reminiscences—were reduced to ashes. With the exception of a narrow strip in the upper part and a few houses over Cedar Creek, near the line of Richland—all of Fairfield has suffered. This plundering, pillaging, house burning horde spread all over the county for a space of forty to fifty miles, exploring field and forest, high lands and low lands, old fields, new grounds, briar thickets and pine thickets, broom grass fields, meadows, gardens, orchards and graveyards. Instead of marching in heavy columns along the highway or in squads along by paths of country roads, as many erroneously conceived they would do, they extended out to right and left irrespectively of roads, taking one broad sweep of the country. No house, however small, obscure or retired in its situation escaped their attention. The cavalry galloped up at full speed, dismounted, rushed into the houses without speaking to anyone or observing any of the civilities of civilized life, went up stairs and down stairs, into garrets, cellars, parlors, closets, family apartments, sleeping rooms, breaking open boxes, chests, drawers, bureaus, trunks, secretaries, desks, sideboards, clothes presses and wardrobes destroying all desirable clothes and stealing blankets and fine quilts, which many cases they put on their sore backed horses, ladies' clothing and gentleman's clothing and elegant wrought pillow cases which they converted into flour bags, sometimes strewing the contents of the bureaus and wardrobes all over the floor and occasionally tearing fine silk dresses into shreds. All decency and civility were ignored. The private apartments of ladies were unceremoniously entered and rummaged and the ladies themselves called by such vile epithets as the Yankee vocabulary contains. Earrings and finger rings, bracelets, in one instance at least, the other jewelry were rudely torn from their person and in some cases by the hands of their own Negro men, who were forced to do it by pistols and bayonets presented to their breasts. In one instance at least, the clothing intended for an unborn infant were taken. Gold and silver and ardent sprits were the most coveted. To the scandal of humanity be it recorded that 11 monuments were searched, graves interrupted and coffins disinterred and broken open in quest of concealed treasure. Horses and mules were driven off. Colts and young horses that could not be caught and bridled were shot down. Fairfield is stripped of horses and mules. With the exception of a few here and there and some broken down and sore backed, emancipated animals left by the invaders, there were no horses in the district immediately subsequent to the departure of the Yankees. There are now some collecting from the adjacent districts. Planters generally have next to no means of making a crop so far as horsepower is concerned. Men who formerly made over 2,000 bushels of corn and 100 bales of cotton are now in condition to do little or nothing on their farms. A few acres of corn, perhaps, are now plated in partially prepared grounds by oxen, feeble army horses and by hoes. The country for the time being is paralyzed.

In absence of soldiers, who are scouring the country in different directions, grass would grow upon some of our highways this summer. Many of the usual operations of the country are for the present suspended. There is little or nothing doing in the shops or tanyards. Some of the customary errands are dispensed with or are performed on foot. Some of the doctors are visiting their patients on foot. Men, who before the invasion were mounted on all occasions, visiting their nearest farms and neighbors as well as the most distant on horses, and ladies who could scarcely visit friends or go to church though ever so near, without a driver, a carriage and all the appurtenances of a fashionable traveling establishment—have to stay at home or become pedestrians. Corn in many instances is carried to mill in small parcels on the shoulders of men, not on the backs of mules or in wagons. We have mentioned the subject of mills, and there are but few of them. With but few exceptions they have fallen victim to the spoilers. All the gin houses were burnt and all the cotton, amounting to thousands of bales. In many instances barns, corncribs and stables, with their contents were burned. Unoccupied dwelling houses were consumed and in quite a frequent number of cases houses occupied by their owners shared the same fate. The premises of Capt. Stitt, William Brice, John Adger, Dr. McMaster, Richard Cathcart and Jas. Turner, and many others those names we are not prepared at present to give, were swept as with the besom of destruction. An aggravating circumstance connected with the case of Mr. Turner was that the mother, a venerable lady of 90 years of age, then on her death bed, had to be carried out of the house to escape the flames. This was done notwithstanding the fact that her situation was made known to the incendiary and earnest pleas were made.

Winnsboro experienced some of the tender mercies of the enemy—marks of the vandals presence are to be seen. Some 24 houses were burned with a considerable amount of cotton and other valuable articles, the sufferers being Dr. Boyleston, John Cathcart, Charles Cathcart, Dr. Aiken, Dr. Lauderdale, Messrs. Wolfe, McCully, Hilliard Elder, Jackson, Cremer, Mrs. Ladd and others. The Episcopal church became a prey to the vindictive spirit. A coffin was exhumed from an adjacent grave and put in an upright position to witness the burning, at these sacrilegious wretches alleged, while secular tunes were being played upon the organ, which was brought out of the house before the fire was put out. While in this connection it might be stated that the brick church on Little River was despoiled of its pulpit, pews, floors and sleepers for the purpose of material to erect a bridge for the use of the enemy over the neighboring stream.

No class of persons escaped without insult and depredation of the Yankees. Neither sex or age, nor condition in life, nor respectability of character, nor eminent public service, nor great moral worth, nor amiableness of temper, nor persuasiveness of address or conversation, nor complexion of political opinions afforded any exemption from rudeness and maltreatment. If you were a high toned secessionist you must be punished for that political crime, your house burnt over your head, your person insulted and your means of sustenance destroyed. If you were neutral in reference to the present war, caring little for either party, you were cursed for your lukewarmness and ridiculed as a drone. If you were a Union man, and expressed your satisfaction in receiving them, you were denounced as a hypocrite and treated as a malefactor. Widows and orphans in destitute circumstances were pillaged of their little all. The Negroes for whose benefit the federals professed to wage this war, were robbed. "Tell not in Gath, publish it not in Ashkelon." Nor was this robbery limited to a few isolated cases. It was perpetrated all over the country. Their shoes were taken from their feet, their coats and shirts from their backs, their hats from their heads, their knives and money from their pockets. An invalid Negro woman of 85 or 90 years of age had her blanket taken off her person while lying in bed.

Gentlemen of the first respectability were collared with rudeness, pushed about over the house and yard, cursed and threatened to be shot, with pistols, pointed and snapped at their heads, while others, one of them being 74 years of age, were actually hung up by their necks by a rope and kept suspended until they were past consciousness.

A clergyman had his premises destroyed with his dwelling house, together with more than two-thirds of his library, consisting of hundreds of volumes of theological, literary, historical, scientific and classical books, reviews, pamphlets, old select newspapers, over a thousand letters received from correspondents in the various parts of the country and some 450 manuscripts, sermons of his own production, pretty fully written out.

The air of decency and refinement much more than that of piety were shocked with the profanity of the federal army. The testimony in the case is, the invaders were horribly shockingly profane.

They cursed in good humor, they cursed in bad humor, they cursed old men and old women, they cursed young ladies, they cursed those who tried to please them and whose who did not try to please them—they cursed white and black, the good and the bad, pouring out their bitter execrations upon all in their presence. In view of these facts is it a wonder that a certain professional gentleman, characterized for modesty of expression, when asked since the invasion by some friend if he had not been visited by rough men (alluding to the federal soldiers) felt it proper to reply in the negative, alleging if he must answer the question that he was visited by a legion of devils, not by men.

Fairfield represents a melancholy spectacle. Ride up the road from Winnsboro to Chesterville and you will see that for the first eight miles the demon of destruction had done its worst. Dwellings houses, gin houses, barns, stables, corn cribs and fences burned; the railroad demolished, dead cattle lying in heaps, dead horses in the road and in the wayside. Go out in the direction of Perry's Ferry, where the main columns of the federal army crossed the river and just such a scene of miles of burnt fencing, of desolated farms, of impoverished plantations, of devastated premises, of shot down horses, cattle and hogs presents itself as a barbarous, uncivilized enemy only can produce.

CHAPTER SEVEN

TIMELINE OF SHERMAN'S SOUTH CAROLINA CAMPAIGN

WHILE SHERMAN'S ARMY was advancing through South Carolina, moving toward Columbia, other Federal troops came up out of the Beaufort area, moving north along the coast toward Charleston in a similarly destructive march. One of the units in this force was the 56th New York Infantry Regiment, actions of which are included in this timeline.

JANUARY 1865

Jan. 2: The 17th Corps of Sherman's army begins making its way from Savannah to Pocotaligo. They have a difficult time crossing the swollen Savannah River into South Carolina.

Jan. 4: A Charleston newspaper reprints part of an editorial that appeared in a northern publication, *The Philadelphia Inquirer* which cheers on Sherman's soldiers as they embark on their South Carolina campaign, and calls South Carolina "that accursed hotbed of treason." Historian John B. Walters commented on this: "This was a strange hatred which directed its venom not against armies but against the non-combatants of South Carolina and their personal property. The people of the North were, in effect, issuing an open invitation to the Union army to sack and pillage the country." While he was in Savannah, General Sherman told some ladies there that he had received letters from the "good, church going people of the North" telling him not to leave a house standing in South Carolina.

Jan. 14: Sherman's forces put the torch to the Episcopal church in Prince William Parish, commonly known as Sheldon Church. Its massive walls still remain today as beautiful ruins, but the interior of the church, and the roof, are burned by enemy troops, just as they were burned by the British during the American Revolution.

Jan. 19: Sherman issues general orders for the march: "Right wing to move men and artillery by transports to head of Broad River and Beaufort; reestablish Port Royal Ferry, and mass the wing at or in the neighborhood of Pocotaligo. Left wing and cavalry to work slowly across the causeway toward Hardeeville, to open a road by which wagons can reach their corps about Broad River; also, by a rapid movement of the left to secure Sister's Ferry (about 40 miles north on the Savannah River), and Augusta road to Robertville." Meanwhile, Dr. Henry Orlando Marcy, a surgeon in a brigade under the command of Colonel Charles Van Wyck, makes observations in his diary about the operations of his brigade in Beaufort District, noting on January 19th that the 56th New York Infantry Regiment burned much of the village of Gillisonville, including the jail, a hotel, several dwelling houses, and a courthouse full of irreplaceable public records. The nearby village of Grahamville was also destroyed at this time. Captain Norman Crossman of the 56th New York also noted the destruction of Gillisonville in his diary on January 19th.

Jan. 23: Sherman arrives at Beaufort by steamer. His troops there manifest much hostility toward the many black people who live in the occupied area of Beaufort.

Jan. 24: Sherman leaves Beaufort for Pocotaligo. The following week, much of the town of Hardeeville is burned, and the rest demolished by Sherman's soldiers. They take apart many of the buildings to make shelters for themselves, and the town's Baptist church is also dismantled. As the church falls to pieces, the soldiers taunt the townspeople: "There goes your damned old gospel shop."

Jan. 31: General Logan's 15th Corps burns the village of McPhersonville, effectively wiping it off the map.

FEBRUARY 1865

Feb. 5: The last of Sherman's troops cross the Savannah River. Soldiers of the 14th Corps burn the entire town of Robertville.

Feb. 7: Forces under the command of General Hugh Judson Kilpatrick burn down most of the town of Barnwell. Some of the infantry troops encamp at the nearby plantation of Mrs. Alfred P. Aldrich. After burning the town of Barnwell, General Kilpatrick jokes that he has changed its name to "Burnwell." Also on February 7, Kilpatrick's cavalry forces arrive at the railroad town of Blackville. The Federal forces destroy over forty major structures in Blackville including the railroad depot and everything connected with it.

Feb. 11: The town of Aiken is the site of a battle which was one of the last Southern victories of the war. Here Confederate General Joseph Wheeler defeats Federal cavalry under the command of General Hugh Judson Kilpatrick. General Kilpatrick's men are forced to retreat, and Aiken is spared the destruction meted out to so many other places in the state. James Courtney, a fifty-four year old civilian who resides near Aiken, is killed by Union troops while trying to save his house from arson.

Feb. 12: About six hundred Confederate soldiers attempt to defend the midlands town of Orangeburg from the onslaught of Sherman's army, but, overwhelmed by a vastly larger force, they are compelled to withdraw towards Columbia, and the Federals cross the Edisto River to take possession of the place. Major Oscar L. Jackson of the 63rd Ohio Infantry Regiment records in his diary that the Federal soldiers who first entered Orangeburg found a store in flames, and claimed it had been deliberately set on fire by its owner, a Jewish merchant. "A fine breeze was blowing," wrote Jackson, "and by the time we got into the town there was a big hole in the center of it and our boys rather assisted [the fire] than stopped its advance." Residents of the town, eyewitnesses, report that they saw a soldier climb up to the roof of Mr. Ezekiel's store and set it on fire with a torch. A young boy named Thomas O.S. Dibble, watching from a nearby window, sees the town's volunteer fire company, a group of old men and boys, trying to put out the flames, and then observes Union soldiers cutting the leather fire hose through which they were pumping water. Before leaving Orangeburg, the soldiers burn down the courthouse there.

Feb. 13: Colonel Oscar Jackson of the 56th New York Infantry Regiment notes in his diary: "Going through South Carolina we are burning nearly all buildings that will burn."

Feb. 14: In her diary, young Emma LeConte, a resident of Columbia, records that there is panic in the city, as Yankees have been reported being on the other side of the river, though how many no one seems to know. Knowing the reputation of Sherman's soldiers, she busies herself making large pockets to wear under her hoopskirt in which to hide valuables. In newspaper articles produced soon after the burning of Columbia, author and historian William Gilmore Simms, South Carolina's foremost man of letters, records that Sherman's forces are about 12 miles from the city at this time. Confederate cavalry under the command of generals Hampton, Wheeler, and Butler are trying to check their progress by skirmishing with them.

Feb. 15: Emma LeConte again records that Columbia is full of panic-stricken crowds trying to escape. "All is confusion and turmoil," she observes in her diary. The government is moving off its stores by train. It is a rainy day. Fighting is still going on outside the city, and Emma writes: "All day wagons and ambulances have been bringing in the wounded over the muddy streets and through the drizzling rain, with dark, gloomy clouds overhead." At night, everyone in the city can hear the sound of cannons, and later the roar of musketry. These sounds grow closer and closer.

Feb. 16: (Thursday) At about 9 in the morning, from the front porch (piazza) of their house, Emma LeConte and her family watch a force of Confederate cavalry passing by on their way to the front. She wrote in her diary: "'Wouldn't it be dreadful if they [meaning the enemy] should shell the city,' someone said. 'They would not do that,' replied Mother, 'for they have not demanded its surrender [yet].' Scarcely had these words passed her lips when Jane, the nurse, rushed in crying out that they were shelling. We ran to the front door just in time to hear a shell go whirring past." Sherman's forces are shelling the city from Lexington Heights. The LeContes take refuge in their basement. The shelling stops a few hours later, but then resumes. At about 10 pm Emma opens a door to find "the atmosphere was stifling with gunpowder smoke."

Feb. 16: William Gilmore Simms notes: "Our troops re-entered the city, burning the several bridges over the Congaree, Broad and Saluda rivers." The shelling continues throughout the day, having begun without any summons for surrender being made, nor any warning given. He also reports: "Numerous shells fell into inhabited portions of the town, yet we hear of only two killed—one on the hospital square." The railroad depot is still crowded, but as

Simms wrote: "The citizens fared badly. The Government of the State and the Confederacy absorbed all the modes of conveyance." Late that night the governor and his staff depart Columbia.

Feb. 16: Most of the town of Lexington, which is very near Columbia, is burned by Sherman's soldiers. According to John Fox, a prominent citizen of the town, Federal forces entered Lexington on February 15. In an affidavit written later, he described what happened to him at his nearby plantation, recording how Federal soldiers robbed him and hung him by the neck with a rope to force him to reveal the whereabouts of other valuables.

Feb. 17: (Friday) At about 6 in the morning, an explosion occurs in the city. Emma LeConte's home shakes, and she thinks a shell has struck it. The South Carolina Railroad Depot has been blown up accidentally by poor people and plunderers who had gone there in search of valuables and food. The looters had taken lamps and torches to light their way, not knowing that kegs of gunpowder were also stored in the buildings, and had caused a massive explosion. The city's firemen soon put out the resulting fires, and afterwards brought out the bodies and remains of more than thirty men and women. There was no way of knowing how many more had simply been blown to bits or incinerated. A little later the cannonading begins again. The air is heavy with smoke. William Gilmore Simms reports: "At an early hour on Friday, the commissary and quartermaster stores were thrown wide, the contents cast out into the streets and given to the people." At 9 am, the mayor of Columbia, Thomas J. Goodwyn, along with two or three aldermen, carries a white flag out of the city and meet with a Colonel Stone of the 15th Corps to officially surrender the city. They are assured by this officer, and later by Gen. Sherman himself, that the city will be safe, and that private property will not be harmed. Some public buildings would be destroyed, they are told, but only after the winds subside, to protect other structures from the spread of any fires that might result.

The Confederate forces reluctantly and sadly withdraw from the city. As some of the Confederates ride out of Columbia, frightened women cry out to them, "What! Leave us! Leave us in the hands of the dreaded foe? Then God have mercy upon us poor helpless deserted women." One of the Confederate officers replies to them that the city has been surrendered, and the army is gone.

Sherman's forces begin to enter the city. They raise the U.S, flag over the state house. Rev. Robert Wilson, an Episcopal clergyman, reports in a letter to a relative that he was in the streets of the city just after Sherman's troops entered the city, and that the soldiers began their pillaging that morning. "Many persons were robbed publicly early in the day," he wrote, adding, "And how shall I attempt to describe the horrors of that fearful night? It is useless to make the effort. Hell was empty, and all its devils were in this devoted city...A perfect reign of terror existed."

Just after noon Sherman and his staff, along with other generals and the 15th Corps, enter Columbia. They are accompanied by numerous bands playing at full blast. One of the songs sung by some soldiers was called "Hail Columbia," and included the following lyrics "Hail Columbia, happy land, if I don't burn you, I'll be damned." Emma LeConte records in her diary that the troops entering the city are accompanied by immense wagon trains. Rev. Peter Shand, an Episcopal priest later wrote a letter in which he recalled of this time: "Soon after [the 15th Corps] was dismissed, they at once spread themselves in every direction...it was not long ere the soldiers commenced the work of pillage, tho' then on a somewhat limited scale—the gigantic and universal sacking of the town being reserved to add to the horrors of the night."

Robberies of citizens by soldiers were common on the streets during the day. William Gilmore Simms wrote of this: "Woe to him who carried a watch with gold chain pendant, or who wore a choice hat, or overcoat, or boots or shoes. He was stripped by ready experts in the twinkling of an eye."

As Sherman's troops enter Columbia, they are offered liquors and wines by many of the black people in the city. Later, some of the Federal soldiers break into stores and businesses to loot valuables and more liquor.

Sherman's soldiers busy themselves by destroying the homes on the outskirts of town and nearby plantations that belong to prominent Confederate citizens. They loot and burn General Wade Hampton's houses and other structures, including the State House, which housed a large library and state records going back to colonial times.

General Oliver Otis Howard, Sherman's second in command, chooses a house on Pendleton Street next to the campus of the South Carolina College (now the University of South Carolina). This house is the home of Mrs. Louisa S. McCord, a widow with two daughters. Just before General Howard arrives, a crowd of Federal soldiers begin ransacking and pillaging the place. One of them seizes Mrs. McCord by the throat, throttles her, and tears a watch from her dress. When General Howard arrives, the soldiers are still at work, and he sees these men in the very act of looting.

A little while later, Howard catches some of his own men attempting to set fire to the McCord residence. Earlier that same day, she had received an ominous note urging her and her family to leave Columbia.

"One of my maids brought me a paper, left, she told me, by a Yankee soldier; it was an ill-spelled but kindly warning of the horrors to come, written upon a torn sheet of my dead son's note book, which, with private papers of every kind now strewed my yard...The writer, a lieutenant of the army of invasion, said he had relatives and friends at the South, and that he felt for us; that his heart bled to think of what was threatened. 'Ladies,' he wrote, 'I pity you; leave this town—go anywhere to be safer than here.' This was written in the morning; the fires were in the evening and night."

Feb. 18: At daylight, the sun rises over a ruined city. Homeless women and children roam and weep among the ruins. One of Sherman's generals wrote of Columbia, "Nearly all the public buildings, several churches, an orphan asylum, and many of the residences were destroyed." The three railroad depots, as well as every house surrounding them, all the stores, several churches, including Christ Church, a synagogue, the Ursuline convent and house, St. Mary's College, hotels, the State House with its great library, and many other buildings—are now an indistinguishable mass of smoking ruins. Other buildings destroyed included the buildings at the Fairgrounds, armories, the Palmetto Iron Works, and the city waterworks.

Feb. 18: Forces under the command of General Hugh Judson Kilpatrick travel to the village of Pomaria Station in Newberry County and destroy it. Pomaria, a well-known, 35 acre plant nursery (one of the finest in the country), is also wantonly destroyed

Feb. 20: Sherman and his troops depart from Columbia.

Feb. 21: Sherman's forces capture Winnsboro in Fairfield District. Between twenty and thirty buildings here are burned, including St. John's Episcopal Church. In an official letter reporting on his division's activities in Winnsboro, Union General W. Geary noted that "acts of pillage and wrong to defenseless inhabitants were committed by foragers...we had daily evidence."

Feb. 21: As the 56th New York Infantry Regiment moves closer to Charleston, Captain Norris Crossman records in his diary that his men have burned the railroad depot at Adams Run, and that they have also burned many houses.

Feb. 22: Captain Norris Crossman's diary records that he and his men marched to Rantowles Station and then encamped at a plantation called Poplar Grove about 10 miles from Charleston. He also reports that dozens of buildings had been burned by his men this day, adding: "in fact, nearly every house on our line of march has been destroyed."

Feb. 23: A Thursday, on which Dr. Henry Orlando Marcy records in his diary that he arrived at Middleton Place, a beautiful estate on the Ashley River near Charleston. Inside the mansion, he finds many fine paintings and a magnificent collection of about 10,000 books that he describes as "the most select private library" he has ever seen. Dr. Marcy "selects" a few of the smaller paintings for himself from the house, but also tries to persuade Major Smith of the 56th New York Infantry Regiment to at least spare the library. Smith orders that Middleton Place be burned and spares nothing. Marcy also reports in his diary (Feb. 24) that the colored people at Middleton place were robbed indiscriminately by the soldiers. Captain Norris Crossman notes in his diary on February 23rd that Major Smith and a party of 100 men marched as far as the Ashley River and "destroyed all the buildings along their route."

Feb. 23: After leaving much of Columbia in ashes in February 1865, Sherman's forces move northward, and at Liberty Hill, South Carolina, General John A. Logan divides his 15th Corps into two columns and sends a detachment from one to raid Camden to the south. The reporter David Conyngham, who was traveling with this detachment, describes Camden as "a beautiful town" and stated that the first Federals to arrive there on February 23 was a small group of "foragers" who "skirmished with some cavalry, driving them into the town, and, following them, soon took possession of it." An article published in the Camden newspaper describes Sherman's soldiers as having "run through the gamut, from impertinence to outrage, from pilfering to wholesale spoliation. Many families have been stripped of everything they had in the world. In one neighborhood, where they unearthed buried liquor, they were especially riotous and fired houses with wanton cruelty."

Feb. 25: Forces under the command of Gen. Hugh Judson Kilpatrick enter and occupy the town of Lancaster. After pillaging many civilians there for a day or two, his men burn most of the town before they leave.

Feb. 26: Captain Norris Crossman of the 56th New York Infantry Regiment records in his diary that he and his men marched into Charleston. "We found the city pretty nearly deserted of white people. The lower end of the town is nearly destroyed by shell and fire."

MARCH 1865

March 5: Sherman's forces arrive in Cheraw, South Carolina. Here they find many goods and supplies which had been sent up from Charleston at the time of its evacuation. Nearly every home and business in Cheraw is robbed of all valuables, and what is not stolen is ruined or destroyed. From Cheraw, the army moves on into the state of North Carolina.

Selected Bibliography

Blease, Cole L. *Destruction of Property in Columbia, S.C. by Sherman's Army*. Washington: Government Printing Office, 1930.

Carroll, James Parsons. *Report of the Committee Appointed to Collect Testimony in Relation to the Destruction of Columbia, S.C., on the 17th of February, 1865*. Columbia, S.C.: The Bryan Printing Co., 1893.

Conrad, August. *The Destruction of Columbia, S.C.—A Translation from the German by Wm. H. Pleasants of the 19th, 20th and 22nd Chapters of "Lights and Shadows in American Life During the War of Secession*. Roanoke, Va.: Stone Printing and Manufacturing Company, 1902.

Dabbs, Edith M. *Sea Island Diary: A History of St. Helena Island*. Spartanburg, SC: The Reprint Co., 1983.

Elmore, Tom. *A Carnival of Destruction: Sherman's Invasion of South Carolina*. Charleston, S.C.: Joggling Board Press, 2012.

Hawks, Esther Hill. *A Woman's Civil War: Esther Hill Hawks' Diary*. Columbia: University of South Carolina Press, 1989.

Jackson, Oscar Lawrence. *The Colonel's Diary: Journals Kept Before and During the Civil War by the Late Colonel Oscar L. Jackson of New Castle, Pennsylvania, Sometime Commander of the 63rd Regiment, O.V.I.* [Sharon, Pa.: 1922]

LeConte, Emma. *When the World Ended: The Diary of Emma LeConte*. New York: Oxford University Press, 1957.

Malone, Linda. *Fairfield Remembers Sherman.* Winnsboro, S.C.: Fairfield Archives and History, 2006.

McCord, Louisa S. *Louisa S. McCord: Poems, Drama, Biography, Letters.* Charlottesville: University Press of Virginia, 1996.

McNeely, Patricia G. *Sherman's Flame and Blame Campaign Through Georgia and the Carolinas.* Columbia, S.C.: McNeely, 2014.

Mehrlander, Andrea. *The Germans of Charleston, Richmond and New Orleans During the Civil War Period, 1850-1870.* New York: DeGruyter, 2011.

Nicholson, William A. *The Burning of Columbia.* Columbia, S.C.: Williams, Sloane, Book and Job Printer, 1895.

Simms, William Gilmore. *Sack and Destruction of the City of Columbia.* Columbia, S.C.: Power Press of Daily Phoenix, 1865.

Stokes, Karen. *Confederate South Carolina.* Charleston, S.C.: The History Press, 2015.

Stokes, Karen. *South Carolina Civilians in Sherman's Path.* Charleston, S.C.: The History Press, 2012.

U.S. Department of War. *The War of the Rebellion: The Official Records of the Union and Confederate Armies.* Washington, D.C.: Government Printing Office, 1880-1909.

The Burning of Columbia. Charleston, S.C.: Walker, Evans & Cogswell, 1888.

Walters, John Bennett. *Merchant of Terror: General Sherman and Total War.* Indianapolis: Bobbs-Merrill, 1973.

Manuscripts

Crossman, Norris. "Norris Crossman Diaries." South Carolina Historical Society.

McCarter Journal, 1860-1866. Library of Congress Manuscript Division.

Marcy, Henry Orlando. "Diary of a Surgeon: U.S. Army, 1864-1865." South Carolina Historical Society.

About the Author

KAREN STOKES has worked with historical manuscripts at the South Carolina Historical Society for over twenty years, and her special area of interest is the Confederate period in the Palmetto State. She is the author of numerous articles and books, and her recent non-fiction works include *South Carolina Civilians in Sherman's Path, The Immortal 600,* and *Confederate South Carolina.* She has also co-edited and published collections of the wartime letters of two Confederate officers, *Faith, Valor and Devotion* and *A Confederate Englishman,* and has authored four works of historical fiction including *Honor in the Dust* and *The Immortals.*

AVAILABLE FROM SHOTWELL PUBLISHING

Non-Fiction:

Punished with Poverty: The Suffering South - Prosperity to Poverty & the Continuing Struggle by James R. & Walter D. Kennedy

Annals of the Stupid Party: Republicans Before Trump by Clyde N. Wilson (The Wilson Files 3)

Nullification: Reclaiming Consent of the Governed by Clyde N. Wilson (The Wilson Files 2)

The Yankee Problem: An American Dilemma by Clyde N. Wilson (The Wilson Files 1)

Maryland, My Maryland: The Cultural Cleansing of a Small Southern State by Joyce Bennett.

Washington's KKK: The Union League During Southern Reconstruction by John Chodes.

When the Yankees Come: Former South Carolina Slaves Remember Sherman's Invasion. Edited with Introduction by Paul C. Graham

Southerner, Take Your Stand! by John Vinson

Lies My Teacher Told Me: The True History of the War for Southern Independence by Clyde N. Wilson

Emancipation Hell: The Tragedy Wrought By Lincoln's Emancipation Proclamation by Kirkpatrick Sale

Southern Independence. Why War? - The War to Prevent Southern Independence by Dr. Charles T. Pace

Fiction:

A New England Romance & Other Southern Stories by Randall Ivey (Green Altar Books)

Tiller by James Everett Kibler (Green Altar Books)

Publisher's Note

IF YOU ENJOYED THIS BOOK or found it useful, interesting, or informative, we'd be very grateful if you would post a brief review of it on the retailer's website.

In the current political and cultural climate, it is important that we get accurate, Southern friendly material into the hands of our friends and neighbours. *Your support can really make a difference* in helping us unapologetically celebrate and defend our Southern heritage, culture, history, and home!

For more information, or to sign-up for notification of forthcoming titles, please visit us at

WWW.SHOTWELLPUBLISHING.COM

Thank You for Your Support!

Made in the USA
Lexington, KY
17 October 2017